Letts

Revise
GCSE

Business
Studies

with Communication Systems

David Floyd

Contents

This book and

STAY ON COURSE!

Use these pages to get to know your course:
- Make sure you know your exam board.
- Know how your course is assessed.
- Check which specification you are doing.

- Find out how your controlled assessment will take place.
- What format are the papers?
- How many papers are there?

	AQA	AQA	Edexcel	Edexcel
Specification name	Business Studies (BS)	Business Studies short course (BS)	Business Studies (BS)	Business Studies short course (BS)
Specification number	4133	4132	2BS01	3BS01
Examination	Two papers 40% and 35%	One paper 50%	Two papers 25% and 50%	One paper 50%
Controlled assessment	25%	50%	25%	50%
Specification Reference Numbers				
Enterprise				
Enterprise and innovation	1.1, 2.1	1.1	1.1, 1.2	1.1, 1.2
The business world				
Business in its environment	1.1, 1.4, 2.1	1.1	1.1, 1.2, 1.3, 3.5	1.1, 1.2, 1.3
The structure of business	1.1, 2.1	1.1	1.4, 3.4	1.4
Business functions				
Marketing and customer service	1.2, 2.2	1.2	1.1, 3.1, 3.2	1.1
Finance in business	1.3, 2.3	1.3	3.3	3.3
People in business	1.4, 2.4	1.4	3.4	3.4
Operations management	1.5, 2.5	1.5	3.2	3.2
Business and communications				
Business communication	N/A	N/A	N/A	N/A
ICT support for business	1.5	N/A	N/A	N/A

(N/A: not applicable to the Specification)

Visit your awarding body for full details of your course or download your complete GCSE specifications.

your GCSE course

OCR	WJEC	CCEA	AQA	Edexcel	OCR
Business Studies (BS)	Business Studies (BS)	Business Studies (BS)	Business and Communication Systems (BCS)	Business Communications (BC)	Business and Communication Systems (BCS)
J253	4080	3210	4134	2BC01	J230
Two papers 25% and 50%	One paper 75%	Two papers 35% and 40%	One paper 40% Computer-based exam 35%	Two papers 25% and 50%	One paper 50% Practical exam 25%
25%	25%	25%	25%	25%	25%

Specification Reference Numbers

OCR	WJEC	CCEA	AQA	Edexcel	OCR
3.1	2.1	3.1	8.1	1.1, 1.2	3.1
3.2, 3.3	2.5	3.1, 3.2	8.1	1.1, 1.2, 1.3, 4.2	3.1, 3.2
3.2	2.1	3.1, 3.2	8.1	1.4, 4.3	3.1
3.1	2.2	3.1, 3.2	8.3	1.1	3.1
3.3	2.6	3.1, 3.2	N/A	1.3	N/A
3.2	2.4	3.1, 3.2	8.1	4.4	3.1
3.3	2.3	3.1	N/A	N/A	N/A
2.2	2.4	3.1	8.1	4.1, 4.2 4.3	3.1, 3.2
2.2	2.4, 2.5	3.2	8.1, 9.1	8.1, 9.1	3.1, 3.2, 3.3

(N/A: not applicable to the Specification)

www.aqa.org.uk, www.ocr.org.uk, www.edexcel.com, www.wjec.co.uk, www.ccea.org.uk

Preparing for the examination

Planning your study

The final months before taking your GCSE examination are very important in achieving your best grade. However, a good grade also depends on you **being well organised** throughout your course.

- After completing a topic in school or college, go through the topic again in the *Revise GCSE Complete Study and Revision Guide*. Copy out the main points again on a sheet of paper, or use a **highlighter pen** to emphasise them.
- A couple of days later try to **write out the key points** from memory. Check any **differences** between what you wrote originally and what you wrote later.
- If you have written your notes on a piece of paper, keep this for revision later.
- **Answer questions** in the *Study Guide* and check your answers.
- Decide whether you have fully **mastered the topic** and write down any weaknesses you think you have.

Preparing a revision programme

In the last three months before the final examination, go through the list of topics in your examination board's specification to **identify those topics you feel the need to concentrate on**. It is tempting to spend valuable revision time on the areas you already know well, but balance this with time spent improving your knowledge of other topics.

When you feel you have mastered all the topics, **spend time attempting past questions**. Each time check your answers with the answers given. In the final couple of weeks **go back and look at your summary sheets** (or highlighting in the book).

How this book will help you

The *Revise GCSE Complete Study and Revision Guide* will help you because...

- it contains the **essential content** for your GCSE course without the extra material that will not be examined
- it contains **progress checks** and exam practice questions to help you confirm your understanding
- it gives **sample GCSE questions** with summary answers and advice from an examiner on how to improve the answer (the questions in this book have been written by an experienced examiner)
- **comments in the margin** and **highlighted key points** will draw your attention to important points you might otherwise miss.

Five ways to improve your grade

Preparation is essential – the following suggestions should point you in the right direction.

❶ Read the question carefully

Many students fail to answer the actual question set. Perhaps they misread the question, or answer a similar one they have studied during revision. To avoid doing this, **read the question right through once**, then **re-read it more slowly**. Some students underline or highlight key words as they read through the question. Questions set for GCSE Business Studies and Business Communications often contain a lot of information, which you should use in your answer by **applying** your knowledge about business studies and communications to this specific information.

❷ Give enough detail

If a part of a question is worth, say, three marks, you should normally make three points: these may be different content points, or you may have to expand and develop a single point. Be careful that you do not make the same point three times because there are **no marks for repetition**.

❸ Quality of your written communication

Some marks on GCSE papers are given for the quality of your written communication. This includes correct sentence structure and correct use of business studies and business communications terms.

❹ Use of business studies and business communications language

There is an important business studies and business communications vocabulary that you should use. Try to use the **correct business or communications terms** in your answers and spell them correctly (including the word 'business' itself!). It is worth using some of your revision time to **make a list of terms** you meet and to check you understand their meanings.

❺ Show workings

It is likely that you will have to do calculations in some questions, for example those that test your knowledge of finance. You should always **show full workings**. Then, if you make an arithmetical mistake, you may still receive marks for correct knowledge.

Controlled assessment

Controlled assessment is the new form of coursework from 2009. Controlled assessment tests your...

- decision-making skills
- ability to analyse and evaluate your work
- research skills
- presentation skills.

The controlled assessment tasks that you do will let you show these skills.

Your controlled assessment topic will be structured by your Examining Group: for example, Edexcel sets the framework for the Business Studies task in Unit 2, and students choose the task they wish to complete with guidance from their school or college.

Here are three key questions for you to ask about your controlled assessment.

❶ Is the organisation or situation I have chosen appropriate?

Teachers sometimes find their students carry out controlled assessments on situations or organisations that are not really appropriate. For example, you might want to study some aspect of a business that interests you (which is a good principle because it will motivate you) - but you must ask questions such as: can I get all the information I need?

❷ Does my topic allow me to demonstrate the right skills?

The main controlled assessment skills are shown above. Whatever your topic, you must...

- obtain information and apply it to your chosen topic
- analyse and judge your information
- summarise and present your findings.

The 'personal' skills you will use include the ability to research, to solve problems, to link different ideas and content, and to persevere with a long-lasting piece of work.

❸ Will it be my own work?

You will not get many (if any) marks for simply copying out lots of information produced by others (e.g. from company brochures and websites). This is the work of others: so, if you include this 'secondary' information you must remember to interpret it and apply it to the situation you are researching.

Remember that although teachers cannot do the work for you, they are able to give you some advice.

1 Enterprise and innovation

The following topics are covered in this chapter:

- Being enterprising
- Franchises
- Innovation
- Business aims, objectives and planning

1.1 Being enterprising

LEARNING SUMMARY

After studying this section you should be able to understand:

- the different meanings of 'enterprise'
- the work of entrepreneurs
- why businesses are started
- the importance of balancing risks and rewards
- skills and qualities that entrepreneurs need

Entrepreneurs

AQA BS	✓
AQA BCS	✗
EDEXCEL BS	✓
EDEXCEL BC	✓
OCR BS	✓
OCR BCS	✓
WJEC BS	✓
CCEA BS	✓

Case study: Hard Bodies

Jen and Owen Evans trained as fitness instructors. They used to work for a large fitness centre but now want to work for themselves. Owen has spotted an opportunity to open a fitness centre in their local town, which at present does not have one. He has rented premises and is installing fitness equipment there. Jen and Owen plan to employ two other fitness trainers to help them in this work and to name the new fitness centre *Hard Bodies*.

When Jen and Owen worked for their last fitness centre, they were given responsibilities for some of the personal training offered at the centre. Both Jen and Owen enjoyed this work. They hope that their new business venture will give them a similar sense of satisfaction and achievement.

Jen and Owen realise they will need a business plan for *Hard Bodies*. At present, Jen has not quite finished this business plan. She realises that the plan needs more information about the expected income from their new business so that they can approach their bank to obtain the finance they need.

Jen and Owen plan to break even in their first year: they hope the income from *Hard Bodies* will cover business costs. They will have to live off savings during this time and then start living off the profits from *Hard Bodies*.

> Make sure you understand the two slightly different meanings of 'enterprise'.

> It helps you to understand what entrepreneurs do if you study a real-life entrepreneur.

What is 'enterprise'? This has two meanings in Business Studies:

- It is another name for a business, such as a company; a business such as *Hard Bodies* can be called an 'enterprise'.
- 'Enterprise' can refer to what business people like Jen and Owen do.

There are many business people in the UK. Well-known business people include Richard Branson with his various Virgin businesses, James Dyson – who is best known for the Dyson vacuum cleaner – and Sir Alan Sugar, who has often appeared on television business and entertainment programmes. They are **entrepreneurs**, people who start a business – and therefore take a financial **risk** – to follow new business opportunities that they hope will lead to **profits** (financial gains) for them.

What does an entrepreneur actually do?

- Starts a business by spotting and following business opportunities.
- Finds and selects people and other resources, and works with them.
- Manages risks and solves problems.

The main reason why an entrepreneur sets up in business is to make profit by selling the business's products. However, some entrepreneurs set up **social enterprises** to trade in goods and services in order to tackle a social or an environmental need. Profit is not the main aim. Examples of social enterprises include *The Big Issue* and the *Eden Project*:

- *The Big Issue* is one of the UK's leading social businesses. It offers homeless people the chance to earn an income by selling the magazine it prints and distributes. The charity part of the business then helps the magazine sellers gain greater control of their lives.
- *The Eden Project* (below) is based in Cornwall and is owned by an educational charity that uses exhibits, events, workshops and educational programmes to remind people what nature gives and to help them learn how to look after nature.

Starting a business

AQA BS	✓
AQA BCS	✗
EDEXCEL BS	✓
EDEXCEL BC	✓
OCR BS	✓
OCR BCS	✓
WJEC BS	✓
CCEA BS	✓

Entrepreneurs show **initiative** by being the first (or one of the first) to carry out a business activity, such as setting up a new shop or making a new product. 'Showing initiative' means that entrepreneurs go ahead and make things happen rather than waiting for things to happen. In the case study on p.9, Jen and Owen are showing initiative by leaving their present employment and setting up a business for themselves.

Entrepreneurs follow new business **opportunities**. Jen and Owen have spotted the opportunity to set up *Hard Bodies* in their local town because there is no competitor there at present. They have established that there is a local **market** – a place where buyers and sellers exchange goods and services – and a **gap in the market**.

Entrepreneurs also find and select **resources** needed in their business, such as people, raw materials, machinery and equipment. Jen and Owen need...
- human resources – by employing other fitness instructors
- physical resources – the new fitness equipment that Owen is installing
- financial resources – Jen and Owen's capital.

Figure 1.1 Resources in business

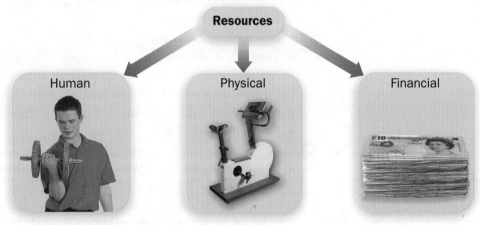

Resources → Human, Physical, Financial

Key questions to ask

Entrepreneurs must ask questions such as 'How?', 'Where?', 'What if?' and 'Why?' so that they can identify possible problems and look at alternatives. Examples of the types of questions that Jen and Owen could ask are:

How	– do we solve any business disagreements we may have? – will we find out about the fitness market in our town?
Where	– can we get business help and advice? – do we buy fitness equipment from?
What	– prices shall we charge? – advertising shall we do?
What if	– one of us becomes ill? – the fitness centre doesn't make any profit?
Why	– do we want to move to these particular premises? – do we offer such a wide range of fitness activities?
Why not	– take on another employee? – open for longer hours on a Sunday?

These and other questions that a potential entrepreneur needs to answer can be grouped under key headings, as follows:

1 What are my reasons?
- **Why do I want to start a business**: is it for profit, for personal freedom and 'escape' from being employed, for enjoyment, or another reason?
- What business and other relevant skills or experiences do I have, and how do I develop these?

2 What is my idea?
- What am I going to do: make goods or provide a service?
  - **goods** are physical things such as televisions, clocks and garden sheds
  - **services** are 'intangible' and non-physical, such as going on a train ride, taking out insurance or watching a TV programme.
- Who will buy it – what age and sex, what income, what lifestyle?
- Who will be my competitors – can I match what they offer?
- How much capital do I have available to risk investing in the business and what other money will I need?
- What sources of business ideas and opportunities do I have? Visits, e.g. trade or industry shows and magazines, visiting the local chamber of commerce; printed sources, e.g. the Yellow Pages and Thomson Local directory, business sections of newspapers; the Internet, e.g. a Google search.

3 What are the requirements?
- What **type of business** will I have: will I run it on my own, will I have a business partner, will I set up a proper limited company, or will I work as a franchisee selling another company's goods or services?
- What **legal**, **tax**, **insurance** and other requirements are there?
- What name will I give to my business?

4 What location?
- What factors will decide where I **locate** my business? For example, where I live; where my customers (the market) and my competitors are; the infrastructure (roads and communications); whether I need to employ people and where they live; what property is available (and do I rent or buy?).

A successful business must be able to meet the needs of its customers

Taking a financial risk

All business opportunities involve risk. Many things can go wrong when starting up or running an existing business. Entrepreneurs cannot accurately judge all business risks because they do not know what will happen in future. For example:
- Am I making enough money from my business? Would I be better off making a safer investment of my **capital** (money invested in the business) by, for example, putting it in a bank or building society savings account?
- Are my business costs – for example, the cost of petrol or power – going to increase in the future so that it is no longer worth me staying in business?
- Will my customers still want my business's products in the future, or will demand for my products die away?
- Will a competitor take actions – such as lowering prices, or setting up in business nearby – meaning that in the future customers will switch to the competitor rather than stay with my business?
- Will the government change a law, e.g. on smoking or drinking, that affects my business (such as a restaurant) and makes it no longer worth me carrying on?

In the case study on p.9, Jen and Owen do not know whether people will like what *Hard Bodies* offers, whether their new employees will like working there, or whether the other fitness centre will drop prices to attract customers to *Hard Bodies'* and make it less likely to give Jen and Owen enough income to live off. If Jen and Owen can overcome problems such as these, their business could be successful. If they cannot cope with these or similar problems, it is likely that *Hard Bodies* will fail as a business.

It is important for entrepreneurs to get a **competitive advantage**: a distinct advantage that a business has, which helps it to do better than the competitors in its market. However, setting up in business is a **calculated risk**. Jen and Owen must balance the risks of the new business against the expected rewards they hope to receive.

The skills and qualities of entrepreneurs

What skills and qualities does an entrepreneur need in order to succeed in business?
- Determination – the ability to see things through to the end and to not let go of a good idea or opportunity.
- Initiative – spotting opportunities and making things happen.
- Honesty – when dealing with other people and businesses, and when judging the position that the entrepreneur's business is in so that sensible decisions are made.
- The ability to plan – for example, by setting business targets.
- Thinking creatively – dealing with problems that arise in an imaginative way, and looking at all options available in any given situation.
- Leadership – to help and inspire others to achieve what is required.

KEY POINT

Entrepreneurs will only be successful if customers want what they offer.

PROGRESS CHECK

1. State three things an entrepreneur does.
2. What are the three main type of resources used in business?
3. What is 'competitive advantage'?

3. An advantage a business has that helps it to do better than competitors
2. Human, physical, financial
1. Start a business, select resources, manage risks.

1.2 Franchises

LEARNING SUMMARY

After studying this section you should be able to understand:

- what franchising is
- the difference between a franchisor and a franchisee
- the benefits of franchising to the franchisor and the franchisee

McDonald's, a Well-known franchise.

The nature of franchising

AQA BS	✓
AQA BCS	✗
EDEXCEL BS	✓
EDEXCEL BC	✓
OCR BS	✓
OCR BCS	✗
WJEC BS	✓
CCEA BS	✓

A **franchise** is the right given by a business to someone who will sell the business's products using the business name. The **franchisor** (the business) grants a license to the **franchisee** (the person operating the outlet), allowing the franchisee to trade using the franchisor's name. The franchisee sells the franchisor's products (goods or services), and is supported by the franchisor's business expertise. In return, the franchisor receives an initial payment from the franchisee and is then paid a regular fee, usually based on a percentage of the **turnover** (sales) or profits that the franchisee makes.

The franchisee owns and controls the business outlet, and the franchisor keeps control over the way the products are marketed and sold, and controls the quality and standards.

Figure 1.1 A typical franchise relationship

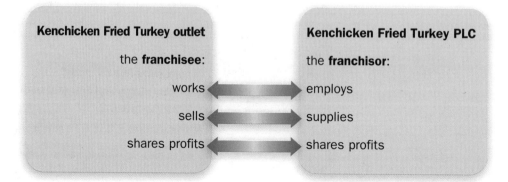

Kenchicken Fried Turkey outlet — the **franchisee**:
works / sells / shares profits

Kenchicken Fried Turkey PLC — the **franchisor**:
employs / supplies / shares profits

The benefits of franchising

For the franchisor...

● the company grows by granting a license to others to sell its product or service
● little investment is needed because the franchisee provides the capital
● fees are received from the franchisee.

For the franchisee, compared with setting up a new business 'from scratch'...

● a new idea is not needed, whereas someone setting up a new business must have an idea for a new product
● the product is already **nationally known** and is **successful**; with a new business, neither the product nor its chance of success is known
● the franchisor has a **good trading name** and might pay for national advertising campaigns; with a new business the owner would have to advertise (locally rather than nationally) and does not as yet have a recognised business name
● franchisors normally offer training programmes in business skills; new business owners need to arrange this for themselves.

Other advantages to the franchisee include...

● possible help from the franchisor to obtain the finance to set up the franchise
● benefits from being part of a large organisation, not only in advertising and training, but also in marketing, product development and management services.

Figure 1.2 Advantages of franchising

'People are increasingly moving into franchising over setting up businesses from scratch – safe in the knowledge that they will be operating under a well-established and trusted brand.'

Keith Davidson, Head of Marketing of Prontaprint (2008)

 From BFA press release 'Franchising: A Success Story in Today's Economic Uncertainty' 10th October 2008

According to the BFA, around £65 000 is the average capital needed to set up a franchise.

There are drawbacks to the franchisee of running a franchise rather than owning the business outright. The initial **costs are high**, and payments such as interest on money borrowed will eat into profits. The franchisee is never in full control because the franchisor decides aspects of the business, such as what products are to be sold and how and where much of the advertising takes place.

KEY POINT

Franchising reduces the risk of business failure because the franchisee is supported by the successful business record of the franchisor.

PROGRESS CHECK

1. Does the franchisor or franchisee work in the franchise outlet?
2. What is one advantage of franchising for the franchisor?
3. How does franchising reduce the risk of business failure?

1. The franchisee 2. **Any one from:** the parent company grows, little investment by franchisor, income is received from the franchisee 3. The franchisee has a successful and known product

1.3 Innovation

LEARNING SUMMARY

After studying this section you should be able to understand:

- what is meant by 'innovation' and Intellectual Property
- the nature and importance of...
  - patents
  - copyright
  - designs
  - trademarks

Innovation and innovators

AQA BS	✓
AQA BCS	✗
EDEXCEL BS	✓
EDEXCEL BC	✓
OCR BS	✓
OCR BCS	✓
WJEC BS	✓
CCEA BS	✓

'**Innovation**' happens when someone turns an idea or an invention into a product that can be sold and a new idea is successfully exploited. Innovation is different from invention. An inventor discovers or creates something new; an innovator turns this new discovery into a saleable product. An **innovator** can be a person, a group of people or an organisation creating this new business idea. Some business ideas are developed by individual innovators who are able to recognise how to change or adapt an existing product, or who spot a gap in the range of products being sold.

Some business ideas are developed in **research departments** set up by larger businesses for this purpose. Any successful products that come from this research will help the business make profits and **stay competitive**. Innovation is therefore a key business process that enables a business to compete successfully in its marketplace. However, the investment that a business makes in researching and developing innovative products is costly and there is no guarantee that the research will lead to successful products.

An example of innovation

amazon.com

Image courtesy of Amazon.com, All Rights Reserved.

Amazon, the internet e-commerce company, was launched online in the USA. It now has separate websites in other countries, including the UK, where it bought an independent online store in 1998 to create Amazon.co.uk.

How is Amazon innovative? Although not the first online store, it is a good example of how an entrepreneur (Jeff Bezos) has developed the idea of the 'virtual store' by striving to meet all the needs of a customer. Amazon does this by not only trying to offer its customers the widest range of goods (new and used) at the lowest possible prices, it also gives them a variety of resources to help make their choice, including customer reviews and personal recommendations.

KEY POINT

The process of innovation involves taking risks.

Inventors and innovators face the risk that someone will copy what they have created, market this copy and therefore compete with them. To stop this happening, businesses can use **Intellectual Property** (IP) to protect their ideas.

IP is created when an idea takes some tangible (physical) form. IP can be legally owned. Inventions (also brands and designs) are examples of IP. There are four main types of IP:

- **Copyright** protects many types of ideas and work, typically involving music, films and broadcasts, and other literary and artistic works. The copyright holder's permission is needed before someone else can use the work in question, otherwise the person using the copyrighted material without permission can be taken to court.
- **Patents** protect inventors. They do this by protecting the features and processes that make things work. The main benefit to a business when taking out a patent is that anyone who copies the business's patented idea can be taken to court. Other advantages for an inventor from taking out a patent include being able to sell or license the invention, or being able to discuss with others how best to set up a business based on the invention.
- **Designs** protect the appearance and appeal of products. A business creating a product with a unique design can seek to register the design and therefore stop anyone from copying it.
- **Trade marks** are brand names and logos. They are distinctive to the goods and services being provided, because they distinguish these goods and services from others. Registering a trade mark gives a business the exclusive right to use it and so stops others using it without permission.

Figure 1.2 Examples of trade marks

> Perhaps the best known example of a trade mark is Coca-Cola.

Trade mark

Copyright

KEY POINT

Intellectual Property rights give protection and therefore reduce risk of misuse.

PROGRESS CHECK

1. What name is given to the department that develops new business ideas?
2. State one risk that an innovator faces.
3. List three ways that intellectual property can be protected.

3. **Any three from:** Register the design, patent, copyright, trade mark
2. Somebody will copy the innovation
1. Research (or Research and Development)

1.4 Business aims, objectives and planning

After studying this section you should be able to understand:

- the nature and purpose of mission statements
- the difference between business aims and objectives
- SMART and non-SMART objectives
- influences on objectives
- the purpose of business planning
- the main sections in a business plan

Mission statements

AQA BS	✓
AQA BCS	✓
EDEXCEL BS	✓
EDEXCEL BC	✓
OCR BS	✓
OCR BCS	✓
WJEC BS	✓
CCEA BS	✓

A **mission statement** summarises the purpose of an organisation (usually a company) by stating what the organisation stands for. The mission statement can sometimes be expressed or expanded in the form of a **vision statement** for the organisation (see Figure 1.3). The mission statement therefore gives people an idea of why the organisation exists and what it seeks to achieve. As a result, all **stakeholders** – groups with an interest in the organisation, such as employees, managers, owners, suppliers, customers and the local community – can understand (and follow) its goals and objectives. The mission statement therefore shows the **core purpose** of the business, i.e. what it stands for.

Figure 1.4 The mission and vision of the BBC in 2009

Mission statements can be found on many company websites.

BBC mission

To enrich people's lives with programmes and services that inform, educate and entertain.

Our vision

To be the most creative organisation in the world.

Business aims and objectives

AQA BS	✓
AQA BCS	✓
EDEXCEL BS	✓
EDEXCEL BC	✓
OCR BS	✓
OCR BCS	✓
WJEC BS	✓
CCEA BS	✓

Aims

Business aims indicate **what the organisation wants to achieve in the long run**. These aims may have both commercial and social influences.

Commercial aims link closely to the business owners, showing what they want from the business. An established and successful company is likely to have business aims such as making a profit, expanding, and selling quality goods, whereas the main aim of a small, recently set up one-person business is likely to be surviving its first year.

Businesses in the **private sector**, such as companies and franchises that are set up to make profits for their owners, have various aims. Their owners will want them to **survive** in the very competitive world in which they operate. If losses are made in the short term, these may be put up with in the hope that business will improve in future. They may also have the aim of gaining a **larger market share**.

> The private sector also includes social enterprises (see page 10)

Growth is an aim closely linked to market share and to survival. Larger businesses are more likely to survive by gaining economies of scale (pages 128–129), and they will have more control of the prices they charge and of their market in general.

Entrepreneurs are in the private sector to make a profit. This **profit motive** encourages people to either invest in existing businesses or to establish themselves in business, perhaps on their own or in partnership with someone. By growing and increasing its market share, the business is more likely to make acceptable profits for its owners.

> The entrepreneur may have a personal desire to see the business grow.

Figure 1.5 The main aims in the private sector

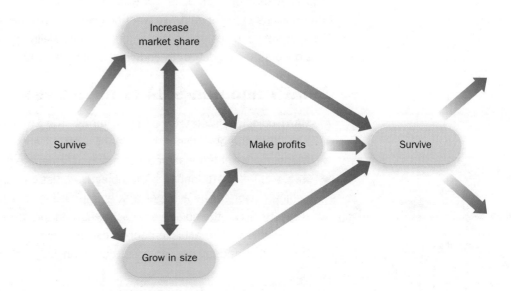

KEY POINT

There are close links between the aims of business.

In addition to the private sector, the UK has organisations in the following sectors:
- **Public sector** – the part of our economy involving the work of central and local government organisations.
- **Voluntary sector** – also called the non-profit sector or 'the third sector' in our economy. Examples include charities, volunteer community organisations and religious organisations.

Many private sector businesses, and organisations in the public and voluntary sectors, have **social aims** that they have established to benefit the local community or society in general. For example, they might set an aim to create local jobs, or to be more environmentally friendly. Organisations that provide community services (such as schools) are likely to have such aims. These organisations might aim to improve the efficiency of the service rather than make a profit, although the need to make profits or surpluses might influence these 'efficiency' aims.

Figure 1.5 Some social aims in 2009

> Oxfam's aim is to get rid of poverty.
>
> (NSPCC) Our purpose is to end cruelty to children. FULL STOP
>
> (Department for Work and Pensions) We are promoting work as the best form of welfare, helping more people into work and supporting those who can't work.

Objectives

Business objectives **explain how an organisation's aims are to be achieved**. Objectives are **shorter term** and can often be measured, so the organisation can check whether it has achieved the objective. Measuring how well an objective has been achieved gives entrepreneurs valuable information and is a key **measure of business success**.

Objectives develop from aims. For example, an aim of the Department for Work and Pensions in 2009 said 'We want children to have the best possible start in life, growing up in secure homes and developing skills for the future.' This is developed as the objective 'to end child poverty by 2020…'

SMART and non-SMART objectives

A SMART objective is stated in 'target' terms. The SMART objective should be…
- **Specific** – the objective states clearly what it wants to achieve.
- **Measurable** – it is measured against a statement (e.g. 'a 10% increase in…').
- **Achievable** (or Attainable) – the objective must be capable of being achieved, not set as a target that is impossible to achieve.
- **Realistic** – can the objective be achieved with the resources that are available?
- **Time-related** – the achievement of the objective must be related to a certain time period or deadline, such as 'this financial year'.

Figure 1.6 Examples of John Lewis's targets

Climate change
- Reduce CO_2 emissions by 10% by 2010 and 20% by 2020, relative to sales
- Aim for 15% reduction in transport CO_2 emmisions from stores deliveries by 2013 (compared with 2005 levels)

Packaging, waste and recycling
- Recycle 50% of all waste by year-end 2010

Objectives personal to the entrepreneur, such as satisfaction, independence and being in control, are non-SMART.

Some objectives are stated in non-SMART (or 'qualitative') terms. For example, a business's objective, based on customer satisfaction, could be SMART if it is stated in measurable terms, such as counting the number of customer complaints made. An example of a non-SMART objective on customer satisfaction is Tesco's 2009 objective of 'offering customers the best value for money and the most competitive prices'.

Influences on objectives

The growth of a business will lead to a change in its objectives. Other influences on objectives come from outside and therefore cannot be controlled. One example is our **economy**: in times of economic growth, objectives based on large profits or increased sales are popular, whereas in a recession the objective of survival is more important.

A business might find that there is **conflict** between objectives. For example, the objective to 'increase profit by 5% this year' conflicts with 'improve employee welfare' because when increasing profits, managers might negotiate lower pay increases. Another conflict is between owners wanting short-term high profits, and managers who want steady growth.

> **KEY POINT**
>
> Detailed objectives will be set for an organisation's main areas or activities, e.g. production, marketing and finance.

Business planning

AQA BS	✓
AQA BCS	✓
EDEXCEL BS	✓
EDEXCEL BC	✓
OCR BS	✓
OCR BCS	✓
WJEC BS	✓
CCEA BS	✓

A business plan is a written document that describes a business, its objectives and strategies, its market and its financial forecasts. The plan is necessary if external finance is needed. The plan also helps establish the resources and finance needed to get started: What marketing? What production? What finance? What resources?

The purpose of planning

A business plan acts as a marketing document to attract potential investors.

Entrepreneurs create a business plan...
- to see **if the business is viable** i.e. whether it is practicable to run the business
- so they can **check the effectiveness** of the business
- to help **raise the finance** the business needs.

The plan must be regularly **updated** because of changes that occur...
- internally, for example, a change in how the factory floor is organised
- externally, for example, changes in tax rates, consumer tastes, or in the strength of the economy.

The contents

Typical sections in a business plan are as follows:

- An **executive summary** – an overview of the new business (some lenders and investors make judgments about the business based only on this).
- A **description of the business** – information on the business and its products, to whom the business will sell, and why it is a suitable idea.
- The **marketing strategy** – why customers are likely to buy the products, and how the products will be sold to them.
- The **management team** – information on the entrepreneur and the staff.
- The **operations** – premises, production facilities, information systems.
- **Financial forecasts** – financial summaries based on the above information.

> **KEY POINT**
>
> The exact content and structure of business plans varies from business to business.

Figure 1.7 Extracts from a hotel's business plan

Executive summary

The Dafydd Hotel overlooks the Irish Sea. The hotel offers seventeen individually furnished rooms, each with its own Welsh theme. Our market strategy is to become the local destination of choice for professional couples who visit this part of Wales and who wish to relax and 'get away from it all...'

Our mission

The Dafydd Hotel intends to provide a relaxed setting for our guests to enjoy the many delights of the beautiful Welsh coast...

Our objectives

To have at least 85% room occupancy each month.
To gain an average revenue of £125 000 per month.
To generate a customer satisfaction rate above 95%.

> **KEY POINT**
>
> Careful business planning helps reduce uncertainty and risk for start-up businesses.

> **PROGRESS CHECK**
>
> 1. What is a mission statement?
> 2. What purpose do business objectives serve?
> 3. What does 'SMART' stand for?
>
> 1. A written document that summarises the purpose of an organisation.
> 2. Targets to achieve by clarifying the mission statement and aims.
> 3. Specific, Measurable, Achievable, Realistic, Time-related.

Sample GCSE questions

This question is based on setting up a new business.

Roz Thomas works in her father's shop. Roz now wants to set up her own shop. Her father's business is a newsagent's and Roz doesn't want to compete with him. The newsagent's used to sell convenience food but no longer does. Roz dealt with the food and plans to set up in business specialising as a café. She considered running a food franchise such as a coffee house, but decided against this. Roz knows that there is only one local competitor. She will compete by offering high quality food and drinks for sale.

(a) Why might Roz have set up in business on her own instead of operating a franchise?

Roz might want greater control over her products and work, and so has decided to set up her own business. **(2)**

> A good point but it could be developed by giving an example of how franchising means less control over 'products and work'.

(b) Why might someone in a similar position decide to work as a franchisee?

Because the franchisor provides support, such as advertising, and the products are likely to be known and successful. Research by Roz shows there is a gap in the local market for a café, although there is one competitor. She has decided to supply food and drinks made with high quality ingredients, and she will therefore charge a high price because of this high quality. **(2)**

> Two relevant points made: a good answer.

(c) Describe one way that the external environment will affect the chance of Roz's business being successful.

Roz faces some competition. The competitor might change the price of the food and drinks being sold to keep customers, and cheaper prices might stop people going to Roz's café, especially because it is likely to charge high prices due to the high quality ingredients. **(2)**

> A detailed and full answer, which uses information given in the question well.

(d) Write a mission statement and a business objective for Roz's new business.

Our mission is to ensure our customers are 100% happy with what they have. One objective is to make profits. **(4)**

> The mission statement can be strengthened by illustrating 'what they have' and using businesslike language: e.g. 'Ensuring that our customers regularly return because they are fully satisfied with the quality of our food and drink, and of our service.' The objective can be made more SMART, e.g. by stating '...making a profit of £5000 in the café's first year of operation.'

Exam practice questions

This is a question on decisions needed when setting up a new business.

1   Ashok trained as a scientist. He works for a large chemical business that creates new substances.

Ashok keeps pets, including two dogs. One day, when out on a walk with his dogs, the collar of one of the dogs snapped. The dog ran on the road and was hurt by a car. Although the dog quickly recovered, Ashok was upset and decided to use his knowledge of materials to prevent this happening again.

Dog collars are usually made from leather or synthetic materials. Ashok has now created a collar made from a special material that will not snap under pressure. He wants to set up his own business in order to make and sell this collar. Ashok realises that he will need to construct a business plan.

(a)   **(i)**   Why does Ashok need to write a business plan?

....

.... **(2)**

(ii) List four sections that are likely to be in Ashok's business plan.

....

....

.... **(4)**

(b)   In addition to writing his business plan, describe two things Ashok must do to set up his new business.

....

....

.... **(4)**

(c)   Outline two types of risk that Ashok faces when running the new business.

....

....

.... **(2)**

(d)   State four skills or qualities that Ashok is likely to need as an entrepreneur.

....

....

(e)   Give one way in which Ashok can stop another business from stealing his invention.   **(4)**

....

....

2 Business in its environment

The following topics are covered in this chapter:

- **Stakeholders**
- **Locating the business**
- **The business environment**
- **The impact of government and international business**
- **Other influences on business**

2.1 Stakeholders

LEARNING SUMMARY

After studying this section you should be able to understand:

- the different types of stakeholders
- the influence of stakeholders

Types of stakeholders

AQA BS ✓
AQA BCS ✓
EDEXCEL BS ✓
EDEXCEL BC ✓
OCR BS ✓
OCR BCS ✓
WJEC BS ✓
CCEA BS ✓

Stakeholders are groups of people or businesses with **interest** in, and an **influence** on, an organisation. Some stakeholders are internal to the organisation and others are external.

> Typical stakeholders own a share in the business or have another financial link with it, work in it or trade with it.

Figure 2.1 The main types of stakeholders

Stakeholder influence

- **Owners** and **shareholders** – the people who have bought shares in the company, who are its owners and who elect the directors – are key stakeholders because they have invested in the business. If owners do not get a good return for their investment, they are likely to end the business and shareholders are likely to sell their shares. These stakeholders want the business to succeed because the better it does, the more money they make.

- **Employees** (including **directors**, who make the major long-term decisions about the company, and **managers**) are key stakeholders because how well they do in their jobs largely decides whether or not the business survives. Businesses want to **motivate** their staff through good pay and working conditions, and let them know what is happening in the business to create loyalty. Employees want the business to succeed: if it does not they will lose their jobs.
- Working closely with **suppliers** means the business can operate efficiently by receiving supplies on time and at a correct price. Suppliers want the business to succeed because if it fails they lose a customer.
- A business can only survive if **customers** buy its goods or services. Customers want the business to succeed because they can keep buying its products.
- **The local community** is interested in the business because it offers them jobs and products and will affect their local environment (for example, by increasing traffic or making a noise). The community wants the business to succeed to preserve jobs in the area.
- **The government** influences all businesses through setting and implementing laws and regulations. The government wants the business to succeed because it pays taxes and creates employment.
- **Lenders** work closely with a business because the business is likely to need to borrow money. Lenders want the business to succeed in order to be paid back the money they are owed.
- **Pressure groups** will be interested in how the business affects their area of interest. For example, a pressure group such as Friends of the Earth will be aware of how the business affects the environment. Pressure groups want a business to succeed because it makes products and creates jobs, but will hope that by doing so the business does not have a negative effect on their area of interest.

Figure 2.2 Tesco's main stakeholders

Here are the main stakeholders we work with:

Customers
Customer Question Time meetings are invaluable. Staff hear customers' views on everything from how we are serving them in our stores to our role in the community.

Staff
Staff give us their feedback through the Viewpoint staff survey, Staff Question Time sessions and our Staff Forum process...

> There will also be conflicts between stakeholders in the public and voluntary sectors.

Stakeholders have a large influence on companies in the private sector. Here, the company's directors have important obligations to their shareholders. One obligation is to make an acceptable amount of profit for the shareholders (who receive it as **dividends** on their shares) to keep the shareholders happy. This **profit motive** may, however, clash with the interests of other stakeholders. For example:

- Customers want high quality and low prices; if the company cuts its prices, this might reduce the profit it makes.
- Suppliers and lenders want the company to be able to pay what it owes them promptly. They are less interested in whether or not the company is making high short-term profits.
- The company's ability to make short-term profit is less important to employees than job security and good pay.
- An environmental pressure group will want environmentally friendly products, which are likely to increase the company's costs and cut into its profits.

PROGRESS CHECK

1. Name two internal stakeholder groups in the private sector.
2. Name two external stakeholder groups in the private sector.

1. **Any two from:** Directors, employees, owners, managers.
2. **Any two from:** Lenders, the local community, government, suppliers, customers, shareholders, pressure groups.

2.2 Locating the business

LEARNING SUMMARY	After studying this section you should be able to understand:
	• historical and modern-day influences on locating a business
	• how the government influences location

Factors influencing location

AQA BS	✓
AQA BCS	✗
EDEXCEL BS	✓
EDEXCEL BC	✓
OCR BS	✓
OCR BCS	✗
WJEC BS	✓
CCEA BS	✓

Many factors influence where a business is located. These factors change in importance over time. For example, modern-day transport and communication systems are more efficient than in the past, and sources of fuel and power have changed. Figure 2.3 shows the various 'pulls' on a business.

Figure 2.3 Influences on where a business locates

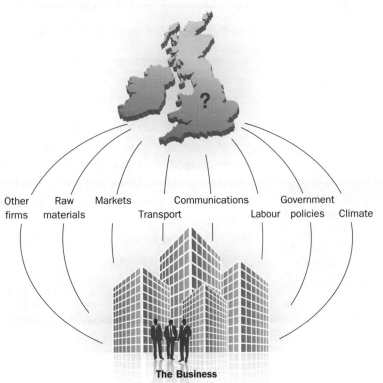

Other firms · Raw materials · Markets · Transport · Communications · Labour · Government policies · Climate

The Business

Historical factors

Many industries grew up near a **supply of raw materials**, such as the Potteries china industry. Availability of fuel, power, water and an appropriate climate were important **natural advantages** in establishing the major cotton and woollen industries that existed in the north of England. These factors are less important now due to improved methods of transport and national availability of modern forms of power, although good climate and soil will always help decide whether an area is used for agriculture.

Modern-day influences

The M4 Corridor is known as the home of the UK's IT industry, having a well-trained and qualified workforce.

- Location near an efficient **transport network** has always been a major influence. Being close to motorway networks, airports and seaports is important when deciding where to locate.
- The entrepreneur will be tempted to locate the business where there is an available and adequately skilled **labour force**. Certain parts of the country may have people with particular knowledge and skills, such as in the Potteries area around Stoke-on-Trent, and in the M4's 'silicon corridor'. The existence of these **external economies** (page 129) encourages new businesses to set up in these areas.

Burton-on-Trent is known for its brewing, and is centrally placed in England to distribute its products.

- As a general rule, if a business's raw materials are bulky and costly to transport, it will want to be located near the source of its materials. If it is a 'weight-gaining' industry (e.g. brewing, where water is added to the raw ingredients) it will locate near the **market** for the finished product in order to save the high cost of transporting the finished goods.

Small-scale businesses with local demand will be located close to their customers.

- The **population** distribution is another influence. Businesses making consumer goods may be tempted to locate near areas of high population, such as south-east England, although the high **cost of land** may discourage them.
- When locating a business, owners have their own likes and dislikes. This **personal choice** is influenced by the personal 'ties' of the entrepreneur.

KEY POINT

The most important factor is how each influence affects the **cost of locating**.

Influence of government

Central government is an important influence in helping decide where businesses are located. 'New towns' such as Telford and Milton Keynes were built with **financial incentives** given to businesses that locate in these areas.

Governments offer companies **grants** (money given to the business), loans (to be repaid), training, improvements to the infrastructure (e.g. roads and telecommunications) and constructing buildings, to encourage them to set up in high unemployment areas. Government aid can come from local authorities, local and regional development agencies, central government and the European Union. Central government has also played a more direct part in locating industry by setting up its own departments outside London, often in areas that are having economic problems.

Examples include the DVLA vehicle licensing centre in Swansea, and the HM Revenue and Customs offices in Newcastle-upon-Tyne.

PROGRESS CHECK

1. List five factors that could influence where an entrepreneur sets up a new business.
2. Give an example of a government activity located outside London.

1. **Any five from:** Climate (agriculture); transport and communication systems; labour supply and skills; closeness of markets; raw materials; government policies; other firms; personal choice.
2. Example: The DVLA in Swansea.

2.3 The business environment

LEARNING SUMMARY

After studying this section you should be able to understand:

- the four factors of production
- influences on production of scarcity, choice and specialisation
- the nature of free market and mixed economies
- the differences between the UK's industrial sectors
- population and employment issues in the UK's economy

Factors of production

AQA BS	✓
AQA BCS	✗
EDEXCEL BS	✓
EDEXCEL BC	✓
OCR BS	✓
OCR BCS	✓
WJEC BS	✓
CCEA BS	✓

Economic activity – activity that seeks to satisfy the needs of the society – takes place within the UK. This means that UK organisations produce goods and services and need resources to do this. These resources are known as **factors of production**.

Figure 2.4 The four factors of production

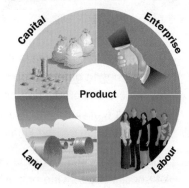

The four factors of production are...

1. **enterprise** – taking the risk of setting up in business
2. **capital** – investment in resources such as machines and equipment
3. **labour** – the number of men and women at work
4. **land** – for purposes such as agriculture and building, and which provides natural resources such as iron ore and other minerals.

> 'Land' also includes the sea and its natural resources, such as fish and oil.

Scarcity and choice

AQA BS	✓
AQA BCS	✗
EDEXCEL BS	✓
EDEXCEL BC	✓
OCR BS	✓
OCR BCS	✓
WJEC BS	✓
CCEA BS	✓

> *In modern economies, employees (labour) have often been replaced by machines (capital) to make production more efficient.

One problem faced by the UK and other countries is that not all the wants of its people can be met. There is not an endless supply of the factors of production – resources are scarce, which means a series of choices have to be made about...

- **what** will be produced – in most cases the **price mechanism** (see page 31) determines this, or the **government** may have a role
- ***how** it will be produced – entrepreneurs combine the factors of production as efficiently as possible
- **where** it will be produced – the availability and position of the factors of production is a major influence in deciding where to produce.

KEY POINT

The UK government's regional policy influences where new businesses are established.

Specialisation

In advanced economies such as the UK's, production tends to be **indirect** – people do not produce things for themselves, but work with others in specialist employment to make goods and services sold to all. They train in different occupations such as teachers, nurses, welders and insurance clerks. Regardless of the jobs they have, people usually have similar wants: for clothes, washing machines, houses, and specialist services such as plumbing or TV repairs. They have to depend on others to provide them with these goods and services.

> Specialising in what we do well leads to greater efficiency and higher output.

Figure 2.5 Specialisation of people

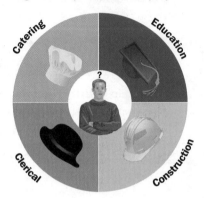

Businesses also specialise: a **division of labour** takes place, with employees specialising in different jobs. This encourages the business to use complex machinery and production processes, with work becoming divided into different business **functions** (the main departments such as Production, Marketing, Human Resources and Finance).

The various 'parts' that make up an economy depend on each other as a result of specialisation. One business depends on another for its 'inputs' or in assisting it to sell its output. For example...

> There are exceptions to this 'rule', e.g. some car manufacturers sell direct to the public through the Internet.

- a farmer specialising in growing vegetables relies on others to distribute, pack and sell these vegetables to the final consumer
- a car manufacturer relies on the expertise of an advertising agency to promote the cars and garages that sell them.

The advantages of specialisation:
- Unit costs are reduced because manufacturing processes are more efficient.
- Specialist equipment is available, leading to quicker and better quality output.
- Employees become specialised and, therefore, more efficient.

The disadvantages of specialisation:
- Boredom for some employees, leading to lower job satisfaction.
- One group of workers taking industrial action can halt production.
- Some employees may possess specialist but out-of-date skills.

Countries also specialise. In many cases, what they specialise in depends on their **climate** and **natural resources**: examples include Bolivia and tin production, Mediterranean countries and tourism, South Africa and gold mining. There may be **historical influences**, such as the development of banking and financial services in the UK. A country is, therefore, not self-sufficient. It has to trade with other countries to get the range of goods and services its population needs but which it cannot provide.

Economic systems

AQA BS	✓
AQA BCS	✗
EDEXCEL BS	✓
EDEXCEL BC	✓
OCR BS	✓
OCR BCS	✓
WJEC BS	✓
CCEA BS	✓

*In a truly 'free' market economy, the government does not interfere in the economy. Resources are owned by individuals and not by the State. The **price mechanism** is its main feature. The prices of goods and services are set by...

- the level of demand for them from consumers
- the willingness of businesses to supply these goods and services.

> *The price mechanism also affects the factors of production, e.g. if the price of labour is too high, it will not be employed.

Features of the free market system

The free market system has the following advantages:

- **Incentive** – the chance of personal wealth encourages people to work hard.
- **Choice** – people can spend their money how they wish.
- **Competition** – inefficient producers are priced out of the market, and more efficient ones supply products at lower prices by using resources more efficiently.

> Recent 'hi-tech' developments, such as advances in mobile phones, are due to the very competitive market.

Figure 2.6 Examples of choice provided by car manufacturers

| Toyota | BMW | Vauxhall |

However, it also has its disadvantages:

- **Unequal distribution of wealth** – wealthier people hold most of the economic and political power, whilst poorer members of society have much less influence.
- **Public services** – the price mechanism doesn't always work efficiently where services such as defence, education and health need to be provided for the benefit of all.
- **Social costs** – because the profit motive is all-important, some businesses ignore social costs of production, such as pollution.
- **Hardship** – in theory, factors of production such as labour are mobile and can change from one use to another; in practice, this is difficult and may lead to hardship through unemployment.

> Businesses value a good public image and are now aware of environmental and other social factors.

KEY POINT

In practice, there are no economies that are entirely 'free market'.

The mixed economy

A **mixed economy** consists of free market activity together with government control. Modern advanced economies such as the UK's are mainly market-based, but there is still a heavy government involvement in areas such as defence and education. In recent years the UK economy has become more market-based through the government **privatising** activities that used to be owned and run by the government.

The government operates the **public sector** (pages 19 and 52), including local authorities and national services such as health. The **private sector** (page 19) is controlled by the price mechanism and 'market forces', although in practice it is **regulated** by various laws.

Education exists in both the private and public sectors

The advantages of the mixed economy are that...

- **necessary services** are provided; in a true market economy, services that failed to make a profit might not be supplied
- **incentive** exists because there is a private sector where individuals can make a lot of money
- **competition** occurs, so prices are kept low.

The industrial sectors

AQA BS	✓
AQA BCS	✗
EDEXCEL BS	✓
EDEXCEL BC	✓
OCR BS	✓
OCR BCS	✓
WJEC BS	✓
CCEA BS	✓

Businesses in advanced economies such as the UK's are involved in production that can be classified under the three headings in Figure 2.7.

The term 'quaternary sector' is sometimes used for businesses involved with information generation and gathering.

Figure 2.7 Types of production

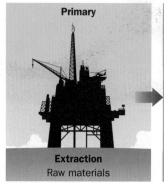

Primary

Extraction
Raw materials

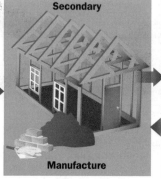

Secondary

Manufacture

Tertiary

Sale
Finished products; Transport

Support
Education; Training; Banking; Insurance

Primary production

Primary production involves the **extraction** of natural resources that become raw materials for other industries. Areas of work in the primary sector of the economy include mining and quarrying, fishing, farming and forestry.

Secondary production

Businesses involved in secondary production take part in either **manufacturing** or **construction**. Such businesses take the outputs of the primary sector and convert them into finished goods that can be sold. Secondary production can be divided into **light industry** and **heavy industry**. Features of the secondary sector are that...

- a finished article is made, such as a car, parts used in assembling other products or buildings, and 'one-off' construction projects such as bridges
- large amounts of energy and resources are used, and waste materials and pollution are common negative by-products.

Tertiary production

In the UK, far more people work in the tertiary sector than in the primary and secondary sectors. The tertiary sector is also known as the **service sector** and supports the primary and secondary sectors. Items that have been grown, extracted, made or built still have to get to the final consumer. Although the producer may sell the items directly to consumers (e.g. a farmer selling farm produce in a farm shop), most products must be transported, stored, advertised, financed and insured. A wide range of commercial services and activities make up tertiary production.

Figure 2.8 Commercial services in the tertiary sector

KEY POINT

The tertiary sector is the dominant sector of the UK economy.

Population and employment

AQA BS	✓
AQA BCS	✗
EDEXCEL BS	✓
EDEXCEL BC	✓
OCR BS	✓
OCR BCS	✓
WJEC BS	✓
CCEA BS	✓

Population

A country's population is one of its most important assets. It provides the economy with the entrepreneurs and labour that produce goods and services. The demand for these products comes from the population. Any change in the population's size or structure will, therefore, affect the economy.

The **age structure** of the UK population is changing. This **changes the demand** for goods and services. For example, an increase in the number of over-60s of retirement age from about one-fifth to about one-third of the total population is predicted in the next 30 years. Another trend is the **movement of labour to the south-east** of the country, encouraged by the opportunity of work but creating the problem of expensive housing and living costs.

> An ageing population increases demand for products such as warmer clothing, smaller houses and flats, and public transport.

Figure 2.9 Expected changes in the UK's population age groups. Source: Office for National Statistics

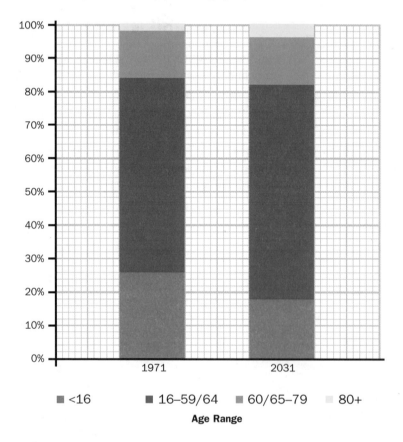

■ <16 ■ 16–59/64 ■ 60/65–79 ■ 80+

Age Range

KEY POINT

Problems of an ageing population include an **increased demand for social services** such as health, and greater **dependence on those in work** to pay the taxes to pay for these social services.

Unemployment

Unemployment has often been a major problem in the UK in recent years. To solve it, the options are to move work to the workers, e.g. government policies that help regions with special difficulties, or to move workers to the work.

Figure 2.10 Headlines about the ups and downs of the jobs market

Jobless rate at 25-year low

Jobs boost for town as company moves in

Jobs are safe in sell-offs

Charity making workers jobless

Vauxhall axes 2,000

BA to shed 1,000 jobs at Gatwick

ICL warns of more jobs to go

Barclays cuts more jobs

With **occupational mobility** of labour, it may be possible for an unemployed person to retrain, change career and find work in the local area. This can prove difficult due to...

- **ability** – an individual may not have the ability or skill to do certain work
- **pay levels** – these may be too low to attract people.

Geographical mobility of labour occurs when people move from one area to another to get work. The main factors that may discourage a person from doing this are...

- **family ties**, such as children at school
- **costs** – high living costs can mean people can't afford to move to where the work is.

> The high cost of living in a region is a problem if the jobs there carry low wages (e.g. some service sector jobs).

KEY POINT

Even prosperous areas of the country such as the south-east have problems, such as traffic congestion and high living costs, which can discourage people from working there.

PROGRESS CHECK

1. Name the four factors of production.
2. What three decisions must be made in an economy?
3. Identify **one** advantage and **one** disadvantage of a free market economy.
4. How does a changing age-profile in the UK affect businesses?

1. Land; labour; capital; enterprise.
2. What to produce; how to produce; where to produce.
3. **Any one from:** Advantages – incentives encourage people to work harder; greater choice; competition leads to invention and innovation. Disadvantages – unequal distribution of wealth; public services can suffer; high social cost; potential hardship through unemployment.
4. It may affect demand for their products, and the supply of their labour.

2.4 The impact of government and international business

LEARNING SUMMARY	**After studying this section you should be able to understand:** ● how the UK government influences businesses by: – its spending and taxation polices – passing laws to protect consumers – ensuring that competition takes place ● the influence of the European Union on UK businesses

Government

AQA BS	✓
AQA BCS	✗
EDEXCEL BS	✓
EDEXCEL BC	✓
OCR BS	✓
OCR BCS	✓
WJEC BS	✓
CCEA BS	✓

All businesses, whether run to make profits for their owners, or to provide a service for the public, are influenced by their external environment.

Figure 2.11 External influences

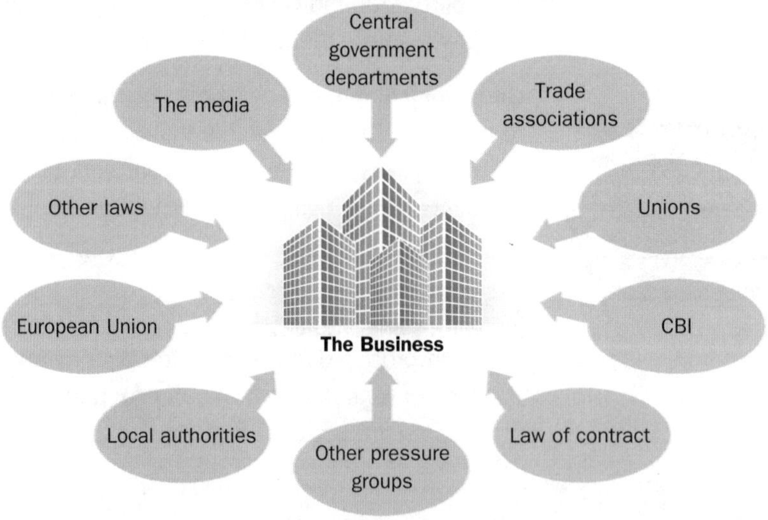

The level of government spending and taxation

Businesses are subject to taxation on profits. Companies pay corporation tax and the owners of businesses not registered as companies will pay income tax. Other costs have to be paid to the government; for example, national insurance is paid by both the employing business and the employee. A business with a large turnover will be VAT registered; this 'purchase tax' is included in the price of many goods.

The level of government spending and taxation affects businesses:
● A change in government spending affects the level of economic activity and, therefore, the amount of work for businesses.
● A change in direct (income-based) tax, such as corporation or income tax, or a change in interest rates, affects the income, cash and profits of businesses.
● A change in the level of indirect tax (VAT) affects the prices charged for goods, and, therefore, affects the level of sales.

Laws that affect business activity

The government tries to ensure that there is no discrimination or other unfair treatment in employment (see page 120) and that employees are protected by health and safety legislation (page 121). It also adopts policies and passes laws for protecting consumers and protecting competition.

Protecting consumers

A **contract** is the legal basis of much that goes on in business. Examples include transactions between two companies, an employee's contract of employment (page 109), and a business selling to a consumer. Most contracts are entered into very easily, for example, over the telephone. Other contracts, for example, to do with buying and selling property, are more formal.

> If a business breaks a contract it might have to pay 'damages' (financial compensation) to the other party.

The government has set up 'watchdogs' to **regulate** (control) organisations. Examples include **OFGEM**, the power regulator, and **OFWAT**, which oversees the water industry.

Figure 2.12 Headlines about regulators at work

The government has passed many **consumer protection** laws that businesses must obey when selling goods or providing services, for example...

> Local authorities also provide consumer protection, such as trading standards and environmental health.

- the **Sale and Supply of Goods Act** – under this Act, goods bought must 'conform to contract', which means that businesses must sell goods of satisfactory quality and are fit for purpose
- the **Trade Descriptions Act** – this makes it a criminal offence for a business to give a false description of its goods or services.

Protecting competition

> The Enterprise Act updated the Fair Trading Act.

The **Enterprise Act** seeks to control abuses that harm customers and fair-trading businesses alike, and to encourage productivity and enterprise. Its measures are enforced by the **Office of Fair Trading** (OFT) which, together with Trading Standards, attempts to stop businesses breaking UK and European consumer protection and competition laws.

> **KEY POINT**
>
> Monopolies, which give the consumer little choice, are discouraged in the private sector because competition should provide consumers with low prices and a greater variety of goods.

The European Union (EU)

AQA BS	✓
AQA BCS	✗
EDEXCEL BS	✓
EDEXCEL BC	✓
OCR BS	✓
OCR BCS	✓
WJEC BS	✓
CCEA BS	✓

Figure 2.13 Headlines about the EU

Euro turns the corner

EU rules blamed for adding £500 to price of a car

Bosses uniting to lobby Brussels

EU funds still misspent, report says

EU bank to bail out tube with £1bn loan

Jobs at risk from EU beet quota proposal

EU told to rise above national interests

The EU influences trading and protects consumers in the UK through various Directives. Examples of its consumer protection include...

- the **Unfair Commercial Practices Directive** (UCPD)
  - the UCPD is implemented in the UK through the Consumer Protection from Unfair Trading Regulations and obliges businesses not to mislead consumers or use commercial practices such as 'high pressure selling'
  - the UCPD applies to all business sectors and will plug gaps in existing UK consumer protection legislation

> The UCPD updates the Trade Descriptions Act.

- the **CE mark**
  - is a declaration by manufacturers that their products meet the relevant European Directives
  - gives businesses easier access into the European market without having to adapt their products.

Figure 2.14 The CE mark

- The EU offers **subsidies**, for example, to those in agriculture through the **Common Agricultural Policy** (CAP). CAP has objectives, such as increasing productivity and ensuring the availability of food, but it has been criticised for harming farmers in developing countries by guaranteeing prices for farmers in the EU.

Figure 2.15 The EU, the UK's main trading partner

Exports 2008

Others	The EU
£9 616m	£11 543m
45.5%	54.5%

Imports 2008

Others	The EU
£13 975m	£14 934m
48.4%	51.6%

- **Free movement of capital and labour** exists in the EU's **Single Market**, which increases trade because there are no internal trade barriers:
  - In the Single Market's areas such as financial services and transport, UK businesses have to compete with other EU businesses.
  - Open markets in areas such as telecommunications have **common standards**, so equipment made by UK businesses must meet these standards.
- Because the EU is a **customs union** – a group of countries with a common arrangement concerning imports from, and exports to, other countries – the EU's **Common Commercial Policy** (CCP) means that goods coming into the EU, wherever they enter, are subject to the same **tariff** (charge) because of the EU's Common External Tariff.

> The EU's Single Administrative Document has simplified paperwork relating to trade in the EU.

KEY POINT

Establishing the Single Market, with features such as the Common External Tariff, has encouraged many overseas businesses to locate in the UK.

The euro debate

The **euro** is the **single currency** used by many EU member states. Although the UK has not joined the euro, UK businesses are still affected, especially those trading in the **eurozone** (the EU member states that have adopted the euro as their official currency).

Figure 2.16 The euro

The euro makes price differences more obvious throughout the eurozone. It gets rid of the need to change currencies, and therefore **avoids exchange rate fluctuations** for exporters and importers.

> Although the euro is not yet used in the UK, more and more businesses now accept it.

Issues for UK businesses include how to handle and record the euro (e.g. in accounts), how to price products for the eurozone, and changing IT and other systems to recognise the euro.

KEY POINT

UK **importers** and **exporters** are most affected by the euro, as are banks and other organisations working in European markets.

International trade

> In 2008, Lloyds TSB expected to pay $350m to the US government and allocated about £170m for this. By 2009, because of the changed exchange rate, the cost had risen to £231m.

When exporting (particularly outside the EU), UK businesses have to cope with...
- the **exchange rates** of currencies – the value of foreign currency bought for £1 can change daily, which makes pricing goods and calculating profits difficult
- differences in **measurements**, such as weights, sizes and electrical voltages
- **language** difficulties, for example, problems of designing sales brochures
- differences in **culture** – what is acceptable in the UK may not be acceptable overseas
- **trading risks** – the risk of granting credit to new overseas clients
- **costs** – higher transport and insurance costs compared with selling in the UK
- **documentation** – complicated procedures outside the EU for the UK exporter.

A government may act to restrict imports into the country. Restricting international trade by using tariffs (see below) can **raise revenue**. The government may seek to **protect existing industries** from competition and to **protect 'infant industries'** that are not yet fully established. It may also wish to **restrict 'dumping'** (foreign goods being exported at extremely low prices by countries wishing to establish a market).

The following are the main types of action normally taken:
- **Tariffs** are import duties, such as the customs and excise duties of the UK, which can be an important source of government revenue. Tariffs raise the price of the imported item, making it less competitive.
- **Quotas** are physical restrictions on the amount of an item imported.
- **Subsidies** are given to home producers, which makes their goods cheaper and, therefore, more competitive than those from importers.
- **Embargoes** are bans on importing certain items, e.g. for political reasons.

KEY POINT

The main disadvantage to a country restricting international trade is that other countries 'follow suit', with the risk of a trade war and an economic recession.

PROGRESS CHECK

1 Give two examples of how the UK government protects consumers.
2 State one way that EU membership affects UK traders.

1. Sale and Supply of Goods Act; Trade Descriptions Act.
2. There are open markets with no trade barriers and free movement of capital and labour.

2.5 Other influences on business

LEARNING SUMMARY

After studying this section you should be able to understand:
- how environmental factors influence business
- the nature of pressure groups
- the role of ethics in business

Environmental Factors

AQA BS	✓
AQA BCS	✗
EDEXCEL BS	✓
EDEXCEL BC	✗
OCR BS	✓
OCR BCS	✓
WJEC BS	✓
CCEA BS	✓

Businesses affect the environment in many ways, using it as a resource by, for example, extracting natural resources, and affecting its quality through activities such as manufacturing and construction.

The UK government helps control the effect that business has on the environment:
- It has a **sustainable development strategy**, so the needs of the present can be met without compromising the ability of future generations to meet their own needs.
- The **Environment Agency** helps regulate businesses by, for example, setting farm waste regulations in agriculture, and regulating the disposal of nuclear waste.
- By law, public limited companies must report on their environmental impact.

In 2007 Marks & Spencer agreed to spend £200m over five years on a sustainable 'eco-plan'.

Figure 2.17 Long-term targets to reduce environmental impact (Tesco, 2008)

The most ambitious target is to halve the carbon footprint of our 2006 estate by 2020. We have also pledged to:

- Build new stores which have, on average, half the carbon footprint of those built in 2006 between now and 2020
- Reduce packaging on all products by 25% by 2010
- Restrict air freighted products to 1% of everything we sell
- Halve emissions from our distribution chain by 2012 per case of goods delivered
- Recycle 80% of store waste by 2010
- Double the amount of customer recycling wherever an automated unit is installed

Pressure groups

AQA BS	✓
AQA BCS	✗
EDEXCEL BS	✓
EDEXCEL BC	✗
OCR BS	✓
OCR BCS	✓
WJEC BS	✓
CCEA BS	✓

In the UK, **pressure groups** – people with similar interests who attempt to influence others – may work locally, such as a local residents' association trying to influence the local council. Many 'cause' pressure groups are national or international, having concerns about human rights, health and environmental matters. Groups such as **Amnesty International**, **Greenpeace** and **ASH** (Action on Smoking and Health) influence businesses by action, such as campaigning for new laws. Other examples include:

- The **Advertising Standards Authority** (ASA) protects consumers by controlling the advertising standards of businesses through its code of advertising practice.
- The **AA** and **RAC** are motoring organisations that campaign on behalf of the motorist.
- **ABTA** – The Travel Association, helps safeguard the holidays of customers who book with one of its member firms by maintaining high standards of trading practice in the industry.
- **Which?** tests goods and services, then reports on them to its members in its series of magazines.
- The **UK media** often carry out investigations on behalf of the public. Newspapers, television programmes such as 'Watchdog', and radio publicise the activities of businesses and individuals who they believe are carrying out unfair or inefficient business practices.

> Pressure groups in the business world include trade unions (see page 121)

Figure 2.18 ABTA and RAC: two organisations that protect consumer groups

Ethics in business

AQA BS	✓
AQA BCS	✗
EDEXCEL BS	✓
EDEXCEL BC	✗
OCR BS	✓
OCR BCS	✓
WJEC BS	✓
CCEA BS	✓

Business ethics concentrates on moral problems that occur in a business. Examples of ethical areas in business include...

- **intellectual property**, such as infringing patents or copyright
- **finance**, for example, areas such as offering bribes or misleading financial information
- **human resource management**, which focuses on areas such as employee privacy and discrimination in recruitment
- **marketing**, which concentrates on aspects such as price-fixing or the content of advertisements
- **production**, which includes how the natural environment is affected.

There are general business ethics such as **corporate social responsibility** (CSR), which examines the relationship that the business has with society.

Figure 2.19 WM Morrisons Plc Corporate Social Responsibility Report 2008/09

Environment
Carbon Footprint – Including energy efficiency and performance, refrigeration, transport and renewable energy.
Waste and recycling – Including carrier bags, packaging, food waste and using waste for renewable energy.

Society
Food specialist for everyone – Including health, safety and wellbeing, skills training, education and customer service.
Engaged and committed workforce – Including training and development to bring the best out of our people.
Community and charity – Including support for local and national good causes; and educational support through our 'Let's Grow' programme.

Business
Closer to source – Including developing relationships with farmers and small producers.
Food quality and safety – Including product integrity, quality and compliance; sampling and residue testing.
Responsible and sustainable sourcing – Including British, local and in-season, animal welfare and fair and ethical working conditions.

KEY POINT

The UK government encourages responsible behaviour by getting businesses to take account of their economic, social and environmental impacts.

PROGRESS CHECK

1. State one way in which the government influences environmental matters in business.
2. What is a 'pressure group'?
3. What does CSR stand for?

1. **Any one from:** It has a sustainable development strategy; it regulates businesses through the Environment Agency, requiring public companies to report on their environmental impact.
2. An organised group of people with similar interests, who attempt to influence others.
3. Corporate Social Responsibility.

Sample GCSE questions

This is a question about the influences of location on a business.

> *Wijetts plc* has been making parts for household 'white goods', such as refrigerators, for many years. The area where the business is located is being redeveloped. The site on which the offices stand has been bought by a retail chain, which plans to build a shopping outlet on the site. *Wijetts plc* will use the finance from selling their site to move to a new location with specially-built premises some five miles away on the outskirts of town.

(a) Examine three factors that the directors of *Wijetts plc* should have considered when searching for a new location.

First, Wijetts must consider the cost of the site, how much it will cost them to stay there.
Secondly, the company needs to check how easy it will be for the present workforce to get to the new site because they will not want to lose staff.
Lastly, the company needs to check how easy it will be for lorries and other transport to get to and from the new site.　　**(6)**

(b) What are the main disadvantages for *Wijetts plc* of moving location?

It will cause everybody a lot of upheaval, so Wijetts must take this into account. It will interrupt production, which could be a problem with lots of orders to meet. Also, it has to tell its customers where it is, and suppliers need to be told too.　　**(6)**

(c) Examine the probable impact of this move on the local community.

The local community will be happy because they will prefer to have a shop rather than a factory on their doorstep.
The traffic may change, from lorries delivering and collecting parts, to cars and taxis delivering and collecting people going to the shop. This could be better or worse, depending on the transport links.
The local community may gain more jobs. Assuming they can get to where Wijetts is moving to, the existing employees can go with Wijetts while the unemployed people living there may have a chance of working in the new shop.[7]　　**(8)**

'Cost' is perhaps the most important factor. You should state the cost 'of' something (the cost of buying the land).

Well explained. Include the knock-on cost of having to recruit new staff.

A good point.

All good points, though 'everybody' is unclear (give examples, such as 'employees').
The points could be developed further, by i) describing the possible problems of being unable to meet orders (loss of income, loss of goodwill, loss of future custom); and ii) extend the final point by thinking about communication, e.g. the need to redesign and reprint stationery, and to check whether phone and fax numbers can be transferred.

A reasonable start. You could mention the likely price rise of homes if a 'nicer' living area is created.

A relevant point: 'infrastructure' is a good word to describe the transport network. Also consider other major social costs or benefits, such as pollution (probably less, although more traffic?).

Another good point: we can also mention the likely differing rates of pay, as well as the different skills required.

Exam practice questions

This is a question on how a business can be affected by changes in the local population.

1. Hadleigh Sports and Leisure Centre is based in a town of approximately 80 000 people. This population is expected to increase by about five percent in the next ten years, and to have a changed age profile as shown below:

Age group	At present (%)	In 10 years (%)
65 and over	17	25
46–64	28	29
26–45	9	22
16–25	21	8
Under 16	25	16

(a) Analyse how these expected changes in age structure could affect the Centre's market.

....

....

....

....

....

....

....

....

....

.... **(8)**

(b) Explain how the Centre might react to these changes.

....

....

....

....

....

....

.... **(4)**

3 The structure of business

The following topics are covered in this chapter:

- Businesses in the UK
- Limited liability companies
- Other forms of private sector organisation
- The public sector
- Internal organisation
- Size and growth

3.1 Businesses in the UK

LEARNING SUMMARY

After studying this section you should be able to understand:

- the difference between the private sector and the public sector
- the difference between unincorporated and incorporated businesses
- the nature, advantages and disadvantages of sole traders
- what a business partnership is
- how limited liability partnerships differ from ordinary partnerships

The UK's mixed economy

AQA BS ✓
AQA BCS ✓
EDEXCEL BS ✓
EDEXCEL BC ✓
OCR BS ✓
OCR BCS ✓
WJEC BS ✓
CCEA BS ✓

The UK has a mixed economy (page 32), the 'mix' being made up of private sector and public sector organisations. The main organisations are shown in Figure 3.1.

Figure 3.1 Business organisations in the UK economy

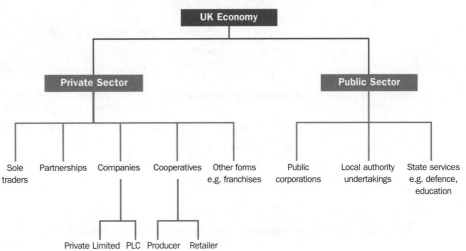

- **Private sector** businesses are owned by individuals. They can be small or large, owned by one person or by thousands. By producing and selling their products, they make **profits** for their owners.
- The **public sector** consists of both central and local government organisations, which provide services for the benefit of the population in general.

Sole traders

Sole traders (also known as **sole proprietors**) are the most common business type in the UK. They are owned and controlled by one person, who often has to provide all the capital required. Formation is easy and the business structure of the firm is usually simple.

Sole traders are **unincorporated** businesses:

- There is **no separate legal existence** from its owners – the business cannot enter contracts in its own name and owners are fully responsible for business debts.
- Sole trader owners have **unlimited liability** for their business debts.
- There are **few formalities** needed to set up as a sole trader.

The government's Small Firms Loan Guarantee scheme helps small and medium-sized businesses obtain loans.

Figure 3.2 Advantages and disadvantages of being a sole trader

Advantages		Disadvantages
Profits are not shared with others.	**BUT**	The owner has **unlimited liability**.
The firm is usually small-scale, so **small amounts of capital** are needed.	**BUT**	Its small-scale nature makes it **difficult to expand**.
The owner is his or her **own boss**.	**BUT**	**Responsibility can't easily be shared**.
Quick decisions can be made.	**BUT**	**Long hours** and **few holidays** are typical.
The business is **easy to establish**.	**BUT**	It can be **difficult to continue** if the owner dies or retires.

KEY POINT

Sole traders can still employ people to work for them: it is the **ownership** that is limited to one person.

Partnerships

A partnership is a business where two or more people work together and share the profits or losses on an agreed basis. Partnerships are easily formed – partners usually draw up a contract called a **deed of partnership** (a partnership agreement) setting out key details.

KEY POINT

Ordinary partnerships are also unincorporated businesses.

Figure 3.3 Content of partnership agreement

AGREEMENT

Names of partners ....

Capital contributed £ ....

£ ....

How profits and losses are shared ....

Partnership salary: £ ....

paid to ....

> One problem is that if a partner leaves or dies, the partnership is ended.

Ordinary partnerships can be formed almost as easily as sole trader businesses. When compared to sole traders, a partnership has a number of advantages:

- Since there will be at least two partners, they can divide control of the business between them (however, disputes may arise between the partners).
- Partners are able to specialise in different business functions.
- Management and responsibility is shared, allowing more time off.
- Partnerships usually have more capital because there are more owners who can contribute. Expansion is therefore easier.

The Limited Liability Partnership (LLP)

> Many lawyers and other professionals have converted ordinary partnerships to LLPs.

Many partners are concerned about unlimited liability. In 2000 the **limited liability partnership (LLP)** was established. The LLP allows the partners to operate as a partnership (profits are still split between them and they pay tax in the normal way), but the LLP is similar to a limited company in that...

- it is a separate legal person (it has to use 'LLP' at the end of its name)
- the LLP is responsible for its business debts.

KEY POINT

Partners in an ordinary partnership, like sole traders, face unlimited liability.

PROGRESS CHECK

1. State two advantages and two disadvantages of a sole trader over a partnership.
2. What does the abbreviation 'LLP' stand for?

1. **Any two from:** Advantages: Sole trader doesn't have to share profit is in total control, only needs small amount of capital, can make quick decisions, business easy to establish. Disadvantages: less capital is normally available, cannot share responsibility, unlimited liability, no one to share responsibility with, long hours and few holidays, difficult to continue if owner dies or retires
2. Limited Liability Partnership.

3.2 Limited liability companies

<table>
<tr><td>LEARNING SUMMARY</td><td>After studying this section you should be able to understand:

• the main features of limited liability companies
• limited company formation
• the private and public forms of limited companies</td></tr>
</table>

Features of limited liability companies

<table>
<tr><td>AQA BS</td><td>✓</td></tr>
<tr><td>AQA BCS</td><td>✓</td></tr>
<tr><td>EDEXCEL BS</td><td>✓</td></tr>
<tr><td>EDEXCEL BC</td><td>✓</td></tr>
<tr><td>OCR BS</td><td>✓</td></tr>
<tr><td>OCR BCS</td><td>✓</td></tr>
<tr><td>WJEC BS</td><td>✓</td></tr>
<tr><td>CCEA BS</td><td>✓</td></tr>
</table>

Limited companies are **incorporated** businesses. They have two key features:

1. ***Limited liability** – the liability of the shareholders who own the company is limited to the value of their agreed investment in the company.
2. **Separate legal existence** from shareholders – a limited company can, in its own name, take legal action, own property and other assets, and enter into contracts. It has **greater continuity** because it is not affected by what happens to an owner (shareholder).

> **Limited liability encourages people to invest because they know there's a limit to the amount they can lose.*

Unlike partnerships and sole traders, where the owners usually run the business, a company's shareholders often have little say in its running. The **directors**, elected by shareholders, control the company; the Board of Directors decides company policies. This **separation of ownership** from control can lead to conflict between shareholder and director objectives.

> *In practice the directors appoint managers to help them run the company.*

Figure 3.4 Different types of company

> *Multinational businesses in the UK usually operate as limited companies.*

Sole trader	Partnership	Limited Companies	
		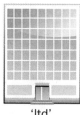 'ltd'	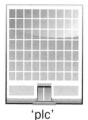 'plc'
Unlimited liability. No separate legal existence		Limited liability. Separate legal existence	

KEY POINT

A limited company must use 'ltd' or 'plc' in its name to **warn** those trading with it that its liability is limited, so they may not be able to recover what is owed if the company cannot meet its debts.

Private limited and public limited

AQA BS	✓
AQA BCS	✓
EDEXCEL BS	✓
EDEXCEL BC	✓
OCR BS	✓
OCR BCS	✓
WJEC BS	✓
CCEA BS	✓

YOUR M&S

Marks and Spencer, a well known Plc

> Be careful not to confuse a public company with the public sector of the economy (page 45).

There are two forms of limited company: **private limited** ('ltd') and **public limited** (plc). Private limited have one or more shareholders; plcs must have at least two shareholders and have issued at least £50 000 shares to the public. The most important difference between them is that **plc shares are quoted** (their price is set and they are traded) on the Stock Exchange.

The main advantage a plc has over a private limited company is that **a plc can raise capital from the public**. It does this by advertising its shares for sale. The other advantages it has tend to come from its **greater size**:

- It is likely to benefit from economies of scale (pages 128–129).
- It is **easier to borrow money** because of its size and the security it can offer.
- Through its size, a plc can specialise more easily.

Plcs also have disadvantages. Its annual accounts are open to public inspection because they have to be published, and the formation of this type of company is more complicated and expensive. Other possible drawbacks for plcs are:

> Compared with a PLC, the ltd is more private because members of the public do not have access to its accounts.

- They may become too large and suffer from **diseconomies of scale** (page 129).
- Ownership can change through **takeover bids** (page 57) launched by a competitor buying the plc's shares.
- The plc may be dominated by institutional investors (businesses such as pension funds and insurance companies).

Figure 3.5 Headlines about takeovers in the news

Thomas Cook is sold to Germans

Focus Do It All takes over Great Mills for £285m

Lloyds TSB offers £20bn for Abbey

French buy Freeserve for £1.65bn

Intec plans to take over one of its US suppliers

News group sold to OK! publishers

Wal-Mart swallows Asda

PROGRESS CHECK

1. State the main difference between a plc and a private ltd.
2. State two main features of being incorporated.

1. plc can apply to the public for share capital; ltd company cannot.
2. A separate legal existence; limited liability.

3.3 Other forms of private sector organisation

LEARNING SUMMARY	After studying this section you should be able to understand:
	• the nature and types of business cooperatives
	• multinationals and their effect on the UK economy

Co-operatives

AQA BS ✓
AQA BCS ✓
EDEXCEL BS ✓
EDEXCEL BC ✓
OCR BS ✓
OCR BCS ✓
WJEC BS ✓
CCEA BS ✓

*Popular areas for worker cooperatives include printing and design, food, and general manufacturing.

*Worker cooperatives are formed for several reasons. Many are new enterprises set up for a niche market; others are where employees buy out the existing employer business, which may have been hit by financial or trading problems. Members contribute the capital and share the profits, usually running the cooperative on democratic lines. Specialists such as accountants may have to be employed.

Retail co-operatives – 'the Co-op' – are well known on the high street. The Cooperative Group operates as a food retailer, pharmacy chain, provider of funeral services, travel, banking and insurance.

Figure 3.6 Aims of the Co-operative Group 2009

The co-operative

Our aims
- to strive for world class levels of business performance
- to be open, responsible and rewarding, putting co-operative values & principles into everyday practice
- to enhance the lives of our people, members, customers, and the communities in which we trade
- to work for the long-term success of the co-operative sector

KEY POINT

Cooperatives can operate as limited companies.

Multinational companies

AQA BS ✓
AQA BCS ✓
EDEXCEL BS ✓
EDEXCEL BC ✓
OCR BS ✓
OCR BCS ✓
WJEC BS ✓
CCEA BS ✓

> Multinationals are responsible for nearly half of all world trade.

The ownership of a multinational company is based in a single country but it **produces in more than one country**.

Figure 3.7 Tesco as a multinational (Source: Tesco plc 2009)

The Group operates in 12 markets outside the UK, in Europe, Asia and North America. Over 160,000 employees work in our international businesses, serving over 28 million customers and generating £13.8 billion sales and over £700 million profit. Over half of our selling space is now outside the UK.

The effect of multinationals on the UK's economy

Multinationals are closely associated with economic **globalisation** – the creation of a single world market. Multinationals bring many benefits to our economy, such as more choice for home consumers, and providing work for local suppliers of goods and services needed by the multinationals. In addition they...

- **reduce unemployment**, e.g. Nissan began car production in north-east England and Toyota did so in the Midlands, both regions having been hit by unemployment
- **introduce new technology and training**, e.g. companies such as Toyota encourage UK competitors to use more modern equipment and training methods.

There are also disadvantages to the UK and other countries as a result of globalisation and multinationals operating in the economy. It may...

> 'Franchises' (page 14) and 'social enterprises' (page 10) are important forms of business ownership.

- **import expertise**, using its own trained managers and employees rather than local ones
- introduce its **own work practices** – these can lead to industrial disputes due to different work practices traditionally being used in the host country
- **send profits out of the country** to its 'home' country
- **exert great influence** over a government's economic policies.

KEY POINT

In the UK, especially since joining the EU and its Single Market (page 39), multinational companies have gained an increasing share of our total production.

PROGRESS CHECK

1. Name the two forms of co-operative organisation.
2. Identify one benefit and one drawback from multinationals operating in the UK.

1. Worker cooperatives and retail cooperatives.
2. **Any one from:** Benefit: increased employment, introduction of new technology and training. Drawback: exporting its profits, import expertise, introduce foreign work practices, introduce foreign work practices, influence government economic polices.

3.4 The public sector

LEARNING SUMMARY	After studying this section you should be able to understand: ● the different types of public sector organisations ● arguments for and against public ownership

Types of public sector organisations

AQA BS ✓
AQA BCS ✓
EDEXCEL BS ✓
EDEXCEL BC ✓
OCR BS ✓
OCR BCS ✓
WJEC BS ✓
CCEA BS ✓

The public sector of the economy consists of those organisations and industries for which **central or local government** is mainly responsible. These are paid for through the taxation system and their purpose is **to provide services for the whole population**.

Figure 3.8 Private and public sectors: the main differences

Sector of the Economy	Ownership	Source of Finance	Reason for Existence
Private Sector	**Private Individual**	**Individuals and Firms**	**Profit Motive**
Sole traders	One person	Sole trader	Profit for owner
Partnerships	Two or more individuals	Partners	Profit for partners
Limited companies	Shareholders	Shareholders Other sources, e.g. commercial banks	Profit for shareholders

Sector of the Economy	Ownership	Source of Finance	Reason for Existence
Public Sector	**Central and Local Government**	**Public Funds**	**Service Motive**
Public corporations	Central government	Taxation and trading	To provide a service, and break even or make profit
Local authority undertakings	Local government	Local finance and trading	To provide a service, and break even or make profit

> A public corporation is quite different from a public limited company.

Public corporations deliver a public service. A board appointed by a government minister decides policy and the government sets financial targets. Examples include British Waterways, which is responsible for managing the UK's canals and waterways, and the Civil Aviation Authority, which provides the UK's air traffic services.

Non-departmental public bodies (NDPBs) work alongside central government, although they are not part of government departments. Examples of NDPBs include the British Museum, the Big Lottery Fund, and UK Sport.

Local authorities run local services such as waste disposal. An authority can operate commercial businesses to raise revenue, which is 'ploughed back' into its services.

During 2008/2009 recession the government has part-nationalised some banks, e.g. Royal Bank of Scotland, as part of its bank 'rescue package'.

Nationalisation – taking private sector businesses into public ownership – was once popular, but in recent years many public sector bodies have been **privatised** (transferred from public to private sector) by the government. Other public services such as transport were either contracted to private sector businesses or **deregulated** (opened up to the private sector) by local councils. It was believed more competition would lead to greater efficiency.

For and against public ownership

The government may decide to take a business or industry into public ownership to...

- **control a natural monopoly**, e.g. ensuring that water is safely purified
- **control a private sector monopoly**, which could otherwise exploit people
- provide **unprofitable but essential services**, e.g. health, education
- **protect an industry** and therefore protect jobs
- **ensure national security** by controlling the armed services.

Public ownership can lead to **inefficiency** since there may be no competition and little incentive to improve efficiency. **Diseconomies of scale** can occur due to the size of the organisations. **Political interference** in the organisations may also take place.

Figure 3.9 The Post Office debate: public or private?

KEY POINT

The argument in favour of public ownership is that the whole population benefits, not simply those who would be able to pay for the public service.

PROGRESS CHECK

1. What is the difference between a public company and a public corporation?

2. State one advantage and one disadvantage associated with public ownership.

1. Public company (plc) seeks to make profits in the private sector; a public corporation is state-owned and provides a service for the public.
2. **Any one from:** Advantage: ensures unprofitable but essential services are provided, control a natural monopoly, control a private sector monopoly, protect an industry, ensure national security; Disadvantage: lack of competition may lead to inefficiency, diseconomies of scale due to size of organisation, political interference can occur.

3.5 Internal organisation

LEARNING SUMMARY

After studying this section you should be able to understand:

● functional and matrix organisation structure
● the purpose of organisation charts
● key terms used to describe organisational structures

Types of structure

AQA BS	✓
AQA BCS	✓
EDEXCEL BS	✓
EDEXCEL BC	✓
OCR BS	✓
OCR BCS	✓
WJEC BS	✓
CCEA BS	✓

*Some businesses, often multinationals, are organised on a 'product' basis, operating as a series of 'divisions' or groups.

**Businesses produce services as well as physical goods.

There is usually a link between an organisation's objectives and its internal structure. *Most private sector businesses are organised by **function**, dividing work into a series of specialist **departments**, for example…

● **accounting and finance** – the finance function obtains and controls business funds
● **marketing** – acts as the all-important link with the business's customers
● **purchasing** – obtains the correct items at the correct times
● **human resources** – the department that looks after employees
● **production** – turns raw material inputs into finished goods output.

Figure 3.10 The departments and structure of a typical manufacturing company

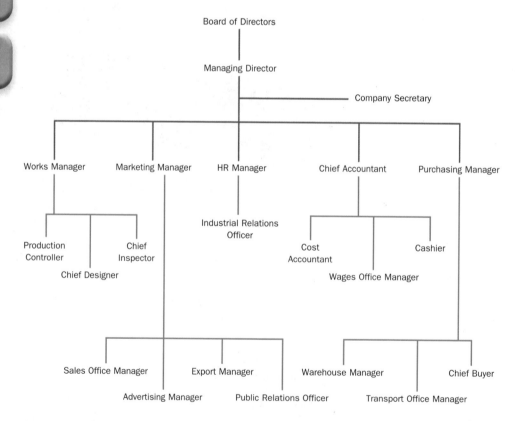

KEY POINT

How a business is organised is largely determined by its objectives.

Some businesses operate partly or wholly using a **matrix** structure, which focuses on business projects or achieving tasks such as **research and development**.

Figure 3.11 Matrix structure for research and development projects

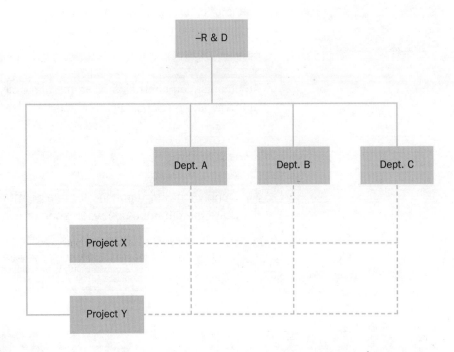

Figure 3.11 illustrates how this business's research and development teams for projects (X and Y) are drawn from three separate departments, these could be, for example, finance, marketing and production.

Organisation charts and terms

An organisation chart displays the **internal structure** of a business. It shows the status of each manager and level, and the **communication lines**. A number of terms are used to describe the key features of an organisation:

- **Span of control** – the **number of employees directly controlled** by someone.
- **Chain of command** – the **status** of different employees, showing who makes decisions and who is responsible to whom.

In Figure 3.10, the Works Manager's span of control is three: the chain of command runs from the Board through the Managing Director and managers to the staff below. Figure 3.10 shows chains of command as a **line authority**, which exist in departments, though the department 'line managers' may be supported by **staff specialists** (e.g. the Company Secretary in Figure 3.10) who advise them.

The normal source of authority comes from the job description (page 106).

The Board and Managing Director do not make all the decisions. They **delegate** (pass down the chain of command) the day-to-day decisions to managers. These managers then delegate the more routine tasks to their staff. Delegation must be accompanied by giving employees **authority** to do the work. The employee then has the **responsibility**. Where there is much delegation, decisions are made at various levels in the business, which is said to be **decentralised**. Where delegation is more limited, higher levels of management keep greater control of decision-making, which is a **centralised** structure.

Many businesses 'flatten' their structure to improve communications and to remove the 'them and us' feeling associated with tall structures.

An organisation's structure may be **tall** or **flat**, indicating the number of levels in the organisation. Tall structures have long chains of command, which normally means...

- communication takes a long time to pass from top to bottom
- spans of control are usually narrow
- employees are usually specialised.

KEY POINT

An organisation chart illustrates the **hierarchy**, the various levels of authority and responsibility that exist.

PROGRESS CHECK

1 Identify four key functions for a large retail organisation.
2 State the difference between span of control and chain of command.

1. Marketing/selling; Accounts; Human resources; Purchasing.
2. Span of control: the number of employees under the direct control of an individual. Chain of command: the line of formal communication in an organisation.

3.6 Size and growth

LEARNING SUMMARY

After studying this section you should be able to understand:

- why and how businesses grow
- how internal growth takes place
- the different forms of external growth

How businesses grow

AQA BS	✓
AQA BCS	✓
EDEXCEL BS	✓
EDEXCEL BC	✗
OCR BS	✓
OCR BCS	✓
WJEC BS	✓
CCEA BS	✓

Businesses grow for a number of reasons. Larger size leads to **economies of scale** (pages 128–129), which make a business more competitive. A larger business usually has a **better chance of survival** through greater market share and borrowing funds more easily. The owners may seek the **power and status** of a larger business.

Business size is measured using **turnover** (sales), **profits**, **capital employed** and **number of employees**.

Businesses in the same industry should be compared using the same measure.

Figure 3.12 Tesco's size, 2008 (source: Tesco financial statements)

Sales	£51.8 billion
Employees	440 000 +
Profit before tax	£2.8 billion
Return on capital employed	12.9 %

Internal expansion

Businesses grow **organically** (naturally) by...
- producing and selling more of their products in their existing markets
- selling their products in new markets
- making and selling new products.

Integration

Integration (external growth) occurs by a takeover or merger:
- A **takeover** is when one company buys enough of another company's voting shares to allow it to take control.
- A **merger** takes place between two companies through agreement. The companies are reorganised following the merger.

Figure 3.12 Headlines about mergers in the news

EMI takes £43m hit for failed merger

Big move in shares amid merger talk

SmithKline and Glaxo near merger go-ahead

Abbey and BoS admit to top level merger talks

Companies merging

Merger mania – coming to a company near you

Shire in £5.9bn merger

Integration by either a takeover or merger allows the new company to expand quickly. There are three forms of integration:
- Horizontal integration.
- Vertical integration.
- Lateral (or conglomerate) integration.

Horizontal integration occurs between **businesses in the same industry** and **at the same stage of production**. An example is Lloyds TSB, which used to be two separate banks.

> Horizontal integration leads to large-scale production and economies of scale, and a larger market share giving greater market power.

Vertical integration takes place between **businesses in the same industry**, but at **different stages of production**. For example, some breweries control their own public houses, and oil companies have their own refineries and filling stations.

A business might integrate with supplier businesses – **vertical backwards** integration – to help control the quality and availability of its supplies. It might integrate with other businesses further along the chain of production – **vertical forwards** integration – to give it better access to its markets.

Lateral integration, also known as conglomerate or diversified integration, occurs when **businesses in different industries** integrate. An example is where tobacco companies, faced with falling UK demand, have taken over other businesses in expanding markets and in doing so reduce the risks of trading in a single uncertain market.

Figure 3.13 The three forms of integration

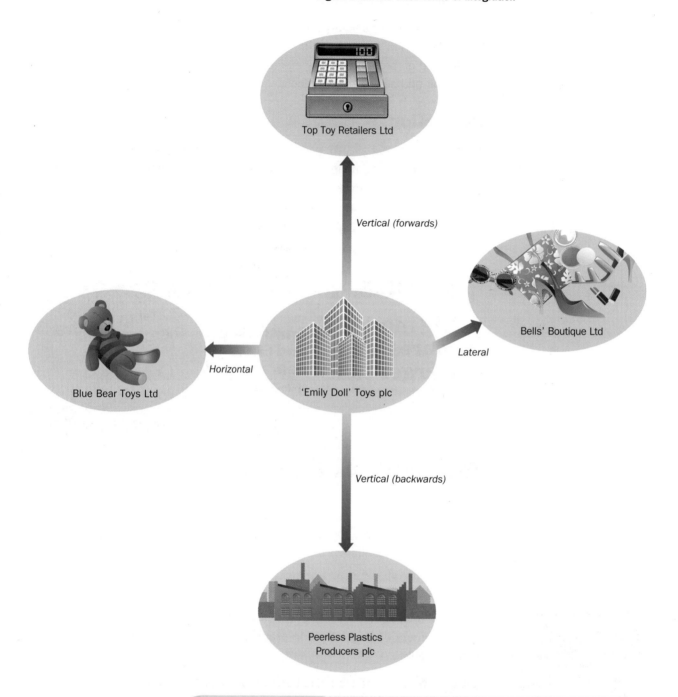

KEY POINT

Businesses often finance internal growth by keeping and using profits.

PROGRESS CHECK

1 List four ways to measure the size of a business.

2 Distinguish between vertical forwards and vertical backwards integration.

1. Turnover; profits; capital employed; employees.
2. Forwards: integration towards the consumer; Backwards: integration towards the point of supply.

Sample GCSE questions

This question is about business objectives and forms of business organisation.

EV plc is a company selling printing franchises. Its directors have two main business objectives: increasing profit and increasing market share.

(a) Explain how *EV plc's* objectives may be linked.

'Profit' is what a company like EV makes when its revenue is greater than its expenses. Market share is EV's share of the market for printing. If EV is making good profits, it can use them to expand its market share. It does this by putting the profits into the company. **(6)**

(b) *EV plc* is also looking for people to take on franchises in their printing business. Laura Lloyd, who already runs her own printing shop as a sole trader, has seen the advertisement and is considering taking on a franchise. The other alternative Laura has considered is to go into partnership with her sister, Emily.

(i) Advise Laura whether she should take on the franchise.

Laura gains from having EV's product, which is probably well known and could be national. She can use EV's expertise as well. The company will provide her with the advice and help she may need. **(4)**

(ii) Explain **one** benefit and **one** drawback to Laura from remaining a sole trader rather than going into partnership with her sister.

By staying a sole trader Laura keeps her independence. This means that she doesn't have to take Emily's views into account when running the business. But if Laura remains a sole trader, she can't get any capital from Emily. **(4)**

(iii) Give **two** reasons why companies such as *EV plc* prefer to expand by franchising rather than through opening their own shops.

EV doesn't have to find the capital to invest, because Laura and the other franchisees will pay it. Secondly, EV doesn't have to take on the full responsibility of running the shops and so on. **(4)**

This is a good start, explaining briefly the terms used in the question.

Again, a relevant and accurate point: you could rephrase 'putting the profits into the company' as 'retaining the profits', and add the point that the company uses the cash kept in the company to help it expand, and therefore increase market share.

Good points, but probably more relevant if Laura didn't already know how to run her business. You need to explain the drawbacks to Laura, for example, loss of independence and having to pay the company out of her profits (or a royalty from her sales).

The benefit could be expanded: you are your own boss through this independence, and so you keep all the profits. The drawback could also be developed by commenting that a lack of capital makes it hard to expand the business.

Well explained: instead of 'and so on', you could give a further example, such as having to find and appoint staff.

Exam practice questions

Here are two questions on forms of business ownership.

1 Which of the following statements apply to public limited companies? **(3)**

A The company can have no more than 20 shareholders	**B** The company cannot sell shares to the general public	
C The company's shares are sold on the Stock Exchange	**D** The company's name is followed by 'ltd'	
E The company is owned by the government	**F** The company has unlimited liability	
G The company must have at least £50 000 share capital	**H** The company's name is followed by 'plc'	

2 Below is a list of features of different types of businesses. Which of these features generally apply to partnerships? Tick the correct options.

A partnership…

A is usually owned by one person ☐

B has unlimited liability ☐

C must put 'plc' at the end of its name ☐

D is owned by shareholders ☐

E is normally in the public sector ☐

F shares the work and profits between the owners ☐

G pays dividends to the owners ☐

H must publish its accounts. ☐ **(4)**

4 Marketing and customer service

The following topics are covered in this chapter:

- Markets
- Pricing decisions
- Place
- The product
- Promotion
- Customers and customer service

4.1 Markets

LEARNING SUMMARY

After studying this section you should be able to understand:

- the meaning of the term 'market'
- consumer and industrial markets
- how markets can be segmented
- how businesses research their markets

Types of market

AQA BS	✓
AQA BCS	✗
EDEXCEL BS	✓
EDEXCEL BC	✓
OCR BS	✓
OCR BCS	✓
WJEC BS	✓
CCEA BS	✓

> We are part of the labour market, selling our qualifications and skills, which are bought by employers.

> TieRack and Sock Shop illustrate how a business can focus successfully on a niche market.

A **market** is when **buyers and sellers are in contact** with each other: it exists where goods and services are bought and sold. We often think of 'the market' as a particular place, such as a group of market stalls selling a range of items. A **specialist market** exists for some products or services, for example, a stock exchange specialises in buying and selling stocks and shares. A market can be local, national or international.

Markets vary in size. A market may be a **mass market**, such as the market for cars. **Niche** markets are also found, for example, the mass market for food contains niche markets based on the different cultural or religious rules associated with certain foods.

Consumer markets supply goods and services to consumers like us. These consist of...

- **single-use goods** such as food or domestic power
- **consumer durables**, e.g. DVD players and washing machines
- **consumer services** such as hairdressers or dentists.

Industrial markets supply the goods and services needed by business, for example...

- **capital goods** (major items such as new machines and equipment)
- **industrial services**, e.g. office cleaning, business stationery printing.

> **KEY POINT**
>
> Customers' wants and needs change all the time and markets respond to these changes.

The marketing mix

A business's market consists of its **actual and potential customers**. To meet customer needs, a business concentrates on its **marketing mix**. It...

- creates its **product**
- sells it at a **price**
- **places** it in the market
- supports it by **promotion**.

Figure 4.1 The marketing mix

> **KEY POINT**
>
> An efficient and appropriate 'mix' of the four Ps – Product, Price, Place, Promotion – should mean that the firm will **survive** and make a **profit** for its owners.

Markets and segmentation

AQA BS	✓
AQA BCS	✗
EDEXCEL BS	✓
EDEXCEL BC	✓
OCR BS	✓
OCR BCS	✓
WJEC BS	✓
CCEA BS	✓

The market for a product can often be broken into different **segments** (parts). For example, the car market in the UK consists of a number of segments. Figure 4.2 shows how the market might be segmented.

Figure 4.2 Market segments

Figure 4.2 shows that businesses can create **particular products for particular segments**. For example, a car manufacturer might target a small hatchback model at the 'second car' segment. By targeting, the business can plan its marketing (such as the advertising campaign) to appeal to customers in these segments.

Each market segment will have its own requirements and will need a different 'mix' of marketing resources. Consumers in markets and segments differ in the following ways:

- **Age** influences product features, such as the way that fashion influences the style of clothes a clothing manufacturer markets.
- **Population** size and geographical distribution influences the marketing of products, for example, decisions on how to transport, where to advertise and where to store the products.
- **Income** influences, for example, the quality of the products marketed and the type of models – 'standard', 'super' and so on – made and marketed.
- **Groupings** – businesses are interested in the various groups in their markets and market segments. Different religious and cultural groupings have their own specialist demand for items, and the number and size of family groups is important to businesses marketing products such as baby clothes and toys.

> The trend towards smaller family units and increased demand for single-person accommodation influences house design and construction.

KEY POINT

Targeting products at distinct market segments allows firms to focus their 'four Ps' (especially promotion) on these segments.

Markets research

AQA BS	✓
AQA BCS	✗
EDEXCEL BS	✓
EDEXCEL BC	✓
OCR BS	✓
OCR BCS	✓
WJEC BS	✓
CCEA BS	✓

*Market research provides **information about the business's market**, such as the likely demand for the products, the types of models in demand, and how the product should be distributed. Managers have the choice of using their Marketing Department or employing a **specialist market research business** such as BRMB or The Nielsen Company.

> *Market research information is important when making decisions about new products or production levels

Primary and secondary research

The main methods of market research are **primary research** and **secondary research**.

Primary	Secondary
• also called field research • obtains new information	• also called desk research • uses existing information

Primary research involves **sampling** a number of likely or actual customers. It uses one or more investigation techniques such as…

- **questionnaires** designed specifically for the task and completed by holding interviews with potential consumers either face-to-face in the street, by telephone, or by post
- **test marketing** – a potential new product is marketed in only one area and reactions to it are studied to see if it should be launched nationally or abandoned
- **consumer panels** – selected people join a panel and are given the product, which they provide detailed comments on.

> Sampling is expensive so a business must balance the cost against the quality of information gained from the sample size.

The main advantage primary research has over secondary is that **it is carried out specifically for the product in question**. Secondary research has been undertaken for other purposes, so its information will not be fully relevant to the business and its product.

A business planning to use **secondary research** has a number of sources:

- **Its own sales information** to identify sales trends and to check consumer suggestions for product changes or requests for new models.
- **Competitors' products** on the market are investigated to discover popular and unpopular features; this helps the business design a better product.
- **Government and other statistics** information, such as trends in spending patterns, population movement and growth, are available in print or online.

Here is an example of government secondary statistics that businesses could use:

Figure 4.3 UK population statistics (source: Office for National Statistics)

Males / Females

NB – data for ages 90 and above are from experimental statistics of the very elderly

Population (thousands)

The resident population of the UK was 60,975,000 in mid-2007. The average age was 39 years, up from 37 in 1997. Children aged under 16 represented around one in five of the total population, around the same proportion as those of retirement age.

Secondary research has two main advantages over primary: it is **less expensive** and is **quicker to obtain** because the information is already available.

KEY POINT

A business's size and resources influence the type and amount of market research it carries out.

PROGRESS CHECK

1. Give three further examples of consumer markets and industrial markets.
2. State four ways in which a market may be segmented.
3. What is the main advantage that field research has over desk research?

1. **Accept any other suitable answers:** Consumer markets for crockery, wallpaper, garden furniture; Industrial markets for accounting software, packaging materials, office desks. 2. Age; Population; Groupings within the population; Disposable income. 3. The information collected relates exclusively to the product being researched.

4.2 The product

After studying this section you should be able to understand:

- the 'product mix' and its analysis
- product life cycles
- how products can be differentiated

The product mix

AQA BS	✓
AQA BCS	✗
EDEXCEL BS	✓
EDEXCEL BC	✓
OCR BS	✓
OCR BCS	✓
WJEC BS	✓
CCEA BS	✓

The range of products a business sells is known as the **product mix**.

Analysing the mix

A popular way to analyse a business's product mix is to use the **Boston Consulting Group's matrix** (grid). This divides products into four categories, according to their market share and the nature of the market.

Figure 4.4 The 'Boston box'

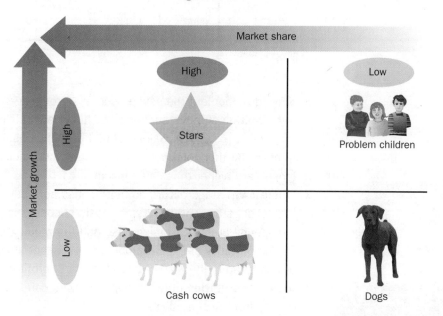

- **Stars** – high market share in a high-growth market. These potentially profitable products still need investment to turn them into 'cash cows'.
- **Problem children** (or 'Question marks') – low market share in a high-growth market. These products may become stars with heavy investment, but are just as likely to turn into dogs.
- **Cash cows** – high market share in a low growth market. These are the main products in terms of profitability and sales.
- **Dogs** – low market share in a low growth market. These are the unprofitable or loss-making products that the business often gets rid of.

KEY POINT

Products in the mix should be **compatible**: they should normally complement (support) each other, not compete with each other.

The product life-cycle

AQA BS	✓
AQA BCS	✗
EDEXCEL BS	✓
EDEXCEL BC	✓
OCR BS	✓
OCR BCS	✓
WJEC BS	✓
CCEA BS	✓

Products have a limited life. New technology, inventions and changes in taste and fashion are examples of factors that affect the length of a product's life.

Although different products last for different lengths of time, their life-cycles have elements in common. This is shown in Figure 4.5 below.

Figure 4.5 Stages of the product life-cycle

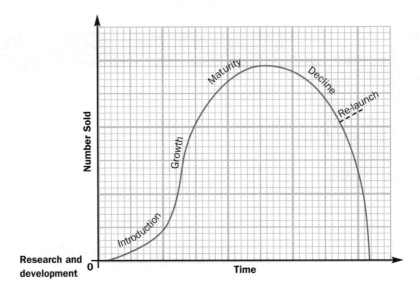

- After development the new product is introduced onto the market. This **introduction** stage is supported by heavy advertising and 'below-the-line' promotion (page 73). Sales will be low until consumers get to know of the product. At this point production costs, which include large development costs, are higher than sales income.
- The **growth** stage occurs as more consumers buy the product, which establishes a **brand loyalty**; its users choose this product rather than a competing brand. Sales increase and the product becomes profitable.
- At the **maturity** stage the product has reached its sales peak, is now fully established in the market and at its most profitable. It may have reached **market saturation** (it has stopped growing) and competitors may have brought out rival products.
- Influences such as the actions of competitors or changes in taste bring the product to the **decline** stage. Sales fall as its market share and influence reduces and it eventually stops being made and sold.

> When watching old films or TV programmes, look out for examples of changes in taste and fashion.

Extending product life

A product's life can often be extended by changing it in some way. A popular method is to **re-launch** products as 'new and improved' models. These **extension strategies** are often linked to changes in packaging, advertising and sales promotion. Methods used to extend product life include adapting it for a new market (e.g. many chocolate bars are now sold in an ice cream format, Figure 4.6), or finding a new use for it, for example, Lucozade was originally sold to help people recover from illness, but is now marketed in 'sports drink' forms.

Figure 4.6 Chocolate bar and Ice cream: extending product life

A business may find it less expensive and safer to extend the life of a well-known and popular product, rather than gamble on producing a new one.

Product differentiation and added value

AQA BS	✓
AQA BCS	✗
EDEXCEL BS	✓
EDEXCEL BC	✓
OCR BS	✓
OCR BCS	✓
WJEC BS	✓
CCEA BS	✓

*A business can identify its USP by completing the sentence 'Customers will buy my product because it is the only…'

A business would like its product to be unique, but usually it has to settle for it being seen as different to competitor's products. This **differentiation** lets the business concentrate on certain aspects of its product, e.g. when advertising it. If the product has a **unique selling point** (USP*), the business will use this to differentiate it. For example, Enterprise Rent-a-Car made its USP 'Pick Enterprise, we'll pick you up', which attracted many customers because they no longer had to drive there since the car was delivered to them.

Product packaging and branding help create differentiation and are important ways in which a business can add value to its products. Originally there to protect a product, **packaging** is now a key element in the marketing mix. The advantage of **branding** is that consumers know the next same-brand product they buy will be almost identical. A company name established by one brand can encourage consumers to buy different products from the same company. For example, Kellogg's is regarded as a quality name in breakfast cereals so consumers may try different cereals carrying the Kellogg's name.

Businesses seek to **add value** to their products through branding, packaging, its USP, and also through its **quality** and by offering **convenience** and **speed** to customers. Adding value generates sales and profits for the business.

Businesses use colour, shape and size to differentiate and market their products.

1. What is the difference between product mix and product differentiation?
2. Name the: (a) stages in the product life-cycle; (b) elements of the 'Boston box'.

1. Product mix indicates the range of product; Products that a business sells; differentiation focuses on how a business creates differences between its products and those of competitors.
2. (a) Introduction; Growth; Maturity; Decline; (b) Stars; Cash cows; Problem children; Dogs.

4.3 Pricing decisions

LEARNING SUMMARY	After studying this section you should be able to understand:
	• the main influences on a product's price
	• high-price, low-price and other strategies used to price products

Influences on price

AQA BS	✓
AQA BCS	✗
EDEXCEL BS	✓
EDEXCEL BC	✓
OCR BS	✓
OCR BCS	✓
WJEC BS	✓
CCEA BS	✓

*Market managers focus more on external market factors, whereas production managers are more influenced by internal production costs.

*The price a business decides on for its product will be influenced by **internal cost-based** and **external market-based** factors. With internal factors, costs of production (pages 87–89) are the main influence. With external factors, competitor prices and the business's position in the market are important.

The business may use **cost-plus pricing** to cover costs, adding on a profit **mark-up**. If the cost of a product is, for example, £2, a mark-up of 50 percent gives a selling price of £3 (and a profit margin of £1). Cost-plus pricing has two main drawbacks: it is not easy to work out accurately the unit cost of production for products, and it ignores competitors' prices and products.

> **KEY POINT**
>
> Break-even analysis (pages 89–92) and marginal costing (page 89) techniques are also cost-based approaches to help decide the price.

Pricing strategies

AQA BS	✓
AQA BCS	✗
EDEXCEL BS	✓
EDEXCEL BC	✓
OCR BS	✓
OCR BCS	✓
WJEC BS	✓
CCEA BS	✓

Examples of premium pricing include 'designer label' clothes.

Games consoles can be cheap when compared with the cost of the games that run on them.

High-price strategies include skimming, maximising and premium pricing.

- A **skimming** strategy is used with a new and unique product; a high price 'skims the cream' (it is also known as **creaming** pricing). Once the 'status symbol' appeal dies down and competitors start selling rival products, the business lowers the price.
- A **maximising** strategy may be used where there is great demand for a product having a short life-cycle. The seller will try to maximise profits by charging high prices.
- **Premium pricing** is used with high-quality products in the market. The business believes consumers will pay for the high quality and prestige (also known as **prestige** pricing) that comes from owning the product.

Low-price strategies include penetration, capturing and loss leader pricing.

- In a **penetration** policy, a low price is set to gain a large market share. Prices may be increased later to earn higher profits.
- A **capturing** price strategy is used where a business makes linked products. For example, it makes both the hardware (equipment) and the software, the hardware having a low price and profits coming from the high-price software.
- A business using the **loss leader** approach sells a product at below cost in order to attract new consumers and increase market share.

Other strategies include…

- **promotional pricing**, where a product's price is reduced for a time in order to promote its sales.
- **odd pricing**, when prices end in odd numbers, for example, 99p, £1.95.
- **psychological pricing** to make the product look cheaper by pricing it just below a 'round figure', for example, £9.95 rather than £10.
- **discrimination pricing**, with different prices for different market segments. For example, public transport has cheaper 'off-peak' fares at set times, and certain groups (e.g. students) can travel the same routes more cheaply than other users.
- **market pricing** or **competitor pricing**, when a 'price taker' sets prices at or near the current market rate.

Figure 4.6 'Odd' and 'psychological' pricing

KEY POINT

Businesses often use a combination of these approaches to pricing, for example, using psychological pricing as part of penetration pricing.

PROGRESS CHECK

1. What is the main internal influence on a firm's price?
2. Name two high-price and two low-price strategies.

1. The full cost of making the product.
2. **Any two from:** High-price: skimming, premium, maximising. Low-price: penetration, capturing, loss leader.

4.4 Promotion

After studying this section you should be able to understand:

- the main methods of promotion
- why and how businesses advertise
- other promotional methods:
  - sales promotion
  - direct marketing
  - personal selling
  - public relations

Businesses and promotion

AQA BS	✓
AQA BCS	✗
EDEXCEL BS	✓
EDEXCEL BC	✓
OCR BS	✓
OCR BCS	✓
WJEC BS	✓
CCEA BS	✓

Businesses promote their products – and themselves – for a number of reasons:

- **Introduce new products to the market**, otherwise people would not know about the product.
- **Increase sales of existing products** – for example, promoting them in a new market.
- **Compete with others** – for example, competing with brands of the same product.
- **Co-operate with others** – such as when a washing powder manufacturer teams up with a washing machine manufacturer.
- **Improve company image** – for example, advertising by some large companies concentrates on its name and image rather than on its products.

Persuasive and informative approaches

> Persuasive promotion is supported by the use of branding, packaging and other forms of product differentiation.

The objective of **persuasive advertising** and other forms of promotion is to **convince consumers that they need the product** for sale.

Informative advertising and other forms of promotion emphasises **full product details** such as technical information. A common example of informative advertising is the job advert section in a local paper.

Figure 4.7 'Persuasive' and 'informative' newspaper advertising

Persuasive

Informative

Methods of promotion

Figure 4.8 below shows that promotion uses four main methods. Sometimes a fifth – public relations – is included.

Figure 4.8 The four main methods of promotion

Advertising

AQA BS	✓
AQA BCS	✗
EDEXCEL BS	✓
EDEXCEL BC	✓
OCR BS	✓
OCR BCS	✓
WJEC BS	✓
CCEA BS	✓

Advertising is called 'above the line' promotion. Advertising has a **sponsor** – the manufacturer or seller of the product – who pays for the advert. It is **non-personal** because it is directed at a mass audience and not an individual (which distinguishes it from personal selling).

Advertising media

> Advertising is called 'above the line' promotion; other methods are called 'below the line'.

The **message** of an advert may be persuasive, informative or both. The **medium** is the method used to communicate this message.

The advantages of advertising in **print-based media** (papers and magazines) are that the advert is **permanent** (it can be cut out and kept or used in some way) and it often gives **more information**, although it **lacks impact** – there is no sound or movement compared with TV and radio broadcast adverts.

- Daily and Sunday newspapers – the 'qualities' such as *The Guardian* and *The Independent* and 'tabloids' such as *The Mirror* – rely on advertising income.
- Regional and local papers are used by sellers with a local (rather than national) demand and market.

> Trade magazine adverts are devoted to particular trades or occupations.

- Free newspapers rely on advertising for their survival. The adverts are usually from local product / service businesses such as garden centres.
- Periodicals and specialist magazines are often 'interest-based', such as sports and hobby magazines; therefore advertisers can target their adverts.

Large businesses selling to a mass market often use **broadcast media**. Adverts tend to be persuasive and can have great impact through the use of **colour**, **sound** and **movement**.

- **Television** adverts reach millions of people and are very persuasive. The adverts are expensive to broadcast, especially at 'peak viewing' times with large audiences, although they can easily be targeted at particular groups and situations (e.g. toy adverts at Christmas).

> Broadcast advertising continues to grow as more cable and satellite channels are set up.

- **Commercial radio** is less expensive for advertisers because of the smaller audience, though its costs vary according to when the advert is broadcast. For example, adverts during peak travel time are often more expensive because many people will be listening in their cars.
- **Websites** and **cinemas** can be used by advertisers, who often target their adverts at certain age groups.

Outdoor media advertising has the advantage of being on **permanent display**:

- **Posters** are often used to sell mass-appeal products. The position of large, permanent poster sites determines how much the poster will cost to display. Posters are also a valuable medium for advertising local events.
- **Illuminated signs** are often used in city and town centres to draw attention to products or locations.

Figure 4.9 The main advertising media

Cinema

Illustration signs

Newspapers and 'free-sheets'

Television

Carrier bags

Magazines

Radio

Leaflets

Posters

Influences on the advertisement

The type of medium and advert are influenced by the following factors:

- **The nature of the product** – industrial market products are often advertised in trade magazines, using an informative approach. Consumer market products often use persuasive techniques and mass media such as television; special interest products are often advertised in magazines dedicated to this interest.
- The position of the product in its **life-cycle** – more informative advertising in the early stages, more persuasive as the product reaches maturity and decline.
- **The target audience** – national adverts for a national audience; informative adverts, perhaps asking the audience to respond in some way, tend to be print-based.
- **The cost** of the advert – the size of the **advertising budget** determines which media the business can afford; designing national adverts can be a specialist activity so many businesses pay specialist advertising agencies to create their adverts.

> **KEY POINT**
>
> **Branding** and **product differentiation** help advertisers promote a product more effectively.

For Advertising		Against Advertising
Information – consumers may not discover the product. **Increased sales** – higher production, more jobs and economies of scale, leading to cheaper prices. **Competition** is encouraged, which should lead to lower prices.	**BUT**	Higher prices if the advertising is unsuccessful. Exploitation – advertising can encourage people to… • buy what they don't need or can't afford • buy products that may be harmful to them, such as alcohol • want more and more material possessions.

Other promotional methods

Other promotional methods are known as 'below-the-line' forms of promotion.

Sales promotion

Sales promotion promotes a product through activities such as displays, exhibitions, demonstrations and shows, and by incentives such as free samples and price reductions. This 'below-the-line' form of promotion directly encourages people to buy.

Point-of-sale (POS) promotion displays, such as 'dump bins' or posters, are in good selling positions (e.g. by the till or at eye level) and **promote the product where it is sold**. POS is often used with low-priced goods such as chocolate because it **encourages impulse buying**.

Consumers may be tempted to buy products, particularly expensive or technologically advanced ones, if the **after-sales service** is linked with the product at the point or time of sale. A **guarantee** relating to after-sale use of the product is often used in sales promotion.

Sponsorship is sometimes used by a business to promote its image and products. For example, tobacco sponsorship has been used widely in some sports (such as Formula 1 motor racing) partly because tobacco cannot be advertised on television.

Trade exhibitions promote the sales of both consumer and industrial goods and bring large numbers of sellers and buyers together.

Sales promotion techniques can be directly linked to the product:
- **Free samples** encourage potential customers to try the product.
- **Price reductions** and **money-off coupons** encourage consumers to buy.
- **Premium offers** offer customers free gifts (e.g. in breakfast cereal packets), or send-away gifts (labels or tokens are collected and sent away).
- **Competitions** encourage people to buy if there is a chance to win a prize.

> Car manufacturers offering three-year warranties on their new cars, compared to others that only offer one year, will promote this difference.

> Cruft's (dog products) and the Motor Show are well-known trade exhibitions.

Figure 4.10 Forms of sales promotion

A sales promotion's effectiveness can be measured by comparing sales before and after the promotion.

Direct marketing

Direct marketing involves selling a product by **approaching consumers rather than selling through retailers**. Forms of direct marketing include...

- **mail order** catalogues, from which customers select and place their orders
- **direct mail** such as 'junk mail' leaflets through the post
- **email**, which is an increasingly popular form of direct marketing.

Personal selling

Personal selling provides special individual information and contact, which other forms of promotion cannot. The business's message is **tailored to the individual buyer**. Sales staff contact the customer, can provide demonstrations and technical information and pass on any sales promotion materials, such as free samples. Sales staff need to be well-trained for personal selling to be effective.

The main advantage of personal selling is the **direct contact** the business has with its customers.

Public relations (PR)

Public relations (PR) is not strictly a form of promotion but can be linked with it.

PR attempts to improve relations between a business and people (who may or may not be its customers). The PR Department uses **press releases** to publicise good points about the business and will be involved with **image marketing**, where the business name and image is promoted as well as its products.

Unlike promotion, PR publicity is not paid for by the business.

PROGRESS CHECK

1. Give three reasons why a business promotes its products.
2. State one argument for, and one argument against, advertising.
3. Name three other forms of promotion.

1. Introduce new products; increase sales of existing products; promote its image.
2. **Any one from: For:** brings products to consumers, attention, increased rates, encourages competition. **Against:** it can exploit consumers, create higher prices.
3. Sales promotion; direct marketing; personal selling.

4.5 Place

After studying this section you should be able to understand:

● the main types of channels of distribution
● the nature of e-commerce

Channels of distribution

AQA BS	✓
AQA BCS	✓
EDEXCEL BS	✓
EDEXCEL BC	✓
OCR BS	✓
OCR BCS	✓
WJEC BS	✓
CCEA BS	✓

Businesses making products for particular markets have to decide how these products will reach their markets. They will make decisions about transport and about the **distribution channels** through which the product will pass.

Wholesalers and retailers

Wholesalers offer services to manufacturers and retailers.

● They **bulk buy** the manufacturer's products – wholesalers are a ready market, and often promote and give information on the products they hold.
● They **break bulk** for retailers – the retailer therefore has lower storage costs and may also be given credit by the wholesaler, which helps finance the purchase.

Figure 4.11 Breaking bulk

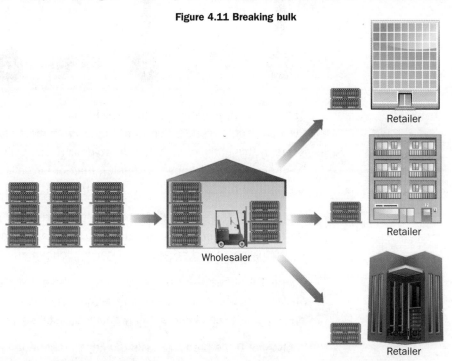

Retailer

Retailer

Retailer

Retailer

Wholesaler

Retailers also provide services to manufacturers and to consumers. Services to manufacturers include **giving information** about product sales and storing the manufacturer's products. Services to consumers can include giving **product advice**, providing **product choice** and a **local outlet**, and offering **credit** and **delivery** services.

Trends in retailing include...

● fewer and larger retail outlets, with the major supermarkets selling an increasingly wide range of goods and services
● an increase in 'own-brand' labels
● greater popularity for out-of-town shopping centres.

The types of channel

Figure 4.12, below, shows the main channels used to pass manufactured consumer goods from producer to consumer. Each channel includes the same activities – as well as being **bought** and **sold**, the product will be **promoted** at the various stages of distribution, **stored** and then **transported** to the next stage.

Figure 4.12 The main channels of distribution

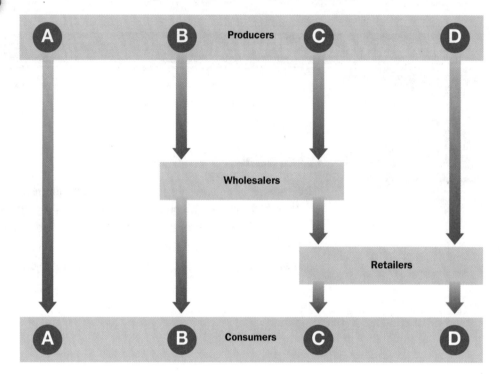

Channel A shows how a producer **sells directly** to the final consumer. For example, some manufacturers run **factory shops** selling their products. Other forms of this channel include **door-to-door** (D2D) selling of products (Avon Cosmetics is a well-known example), **mail order** selling by agents, and farmers selling their produce in farm shops or through 'pick-your-own' offers.

In **channel B** the wholesaler receives goods from the producer and sells them to the final consumer; the retailer is omitted. These wholesalers are usually based in densely-populated areas, often selling consumer durables at low prices.

Channel C shows the traditional pattern where the manufacturer sells in bulk to wholesalers, who then re-sell in smaller quantities to retailers. These retailers then sell single items to consumers. Many goods are still sold using this traditional channel.

In **channel D** the producer sells directly to large retailers such as Tesco and B&Q, who, through their size, organise their own distribution and carry out some of the functions of a wholesaler, such as storing large quantities of goods. Other forms of channel D are producers having their own retail outlets – **vertical forwards integration**, for example farmers selling at a farmers market, (pages 57–58) – and the **franchising** (page 14) of retail outlets.

KEY POINT

Retailers must consider the risk of a product not selling and the space it occupies before stocking a product.

Selecting the channel

The channel used largely depends on the product that is being distributed:

- **Finished consumer goods** use the channels described on page 76, but **raw materials** are often distributed through **commodity exchanges**, for example, the London Metal Exchange is a leading market for a range of metals.
- Some **foodstuffs** are sold at commodity exchanges, through wholesale markets for fresh produce, or by specialist marketing and distribution boards.
- **Industrial goods** are sold using different channels. There may be direct selling by the sales force to the customer, or manufacturers' agents may be used to distribute industrial goods such as farm machinery and steel.

> **KEY POINT**
>
> When deciding on the channel to use, the manufacturer considers its **cost** and the amount of **control** needed over distribution.

E-commerce

AQA BS	✓
AQA BCS	✓
EDEXCEL BS	✓
EDEXCEL BC	✓
OCR BS	✓
OCR BCS	✓
WJEC BS	✓
CCEA BS	✓

E-commerce has become increasingly important as a means for businesses, both large and small, to sell their products.

**Figure 4.13 Sainsbury's interest in e-commerce
(Source: Sainsbury's Group Chief Executive's Review, 2000)**

'One strategic objective is to increase our e-commerce activities ... In June Sainsbury's Supermarkets will launch a major website, *Taste for Life*, which will be a huge source of recipe ideas and product information for customers ... Sainsbury's new upgraded home delivery and Internet shopping service *Sainsbury's to You* ... We are taking the opportunities of e-commerce very seriously ... We are giving a lot of thought to the implications of the growth of Internet shopping on the kind of stores that we operate and what customers will be looking for.'

**Figure 4.14 Sainsbury's development of e-commerce.
(Source: Sainsbury's Annual Report 2008)**

We also continue to extend our relationship with customers beyond the traditional supermarket environment through the growth of our convenience store operation, our online offer and Sainsbury's Bank. We have also announced plans to launch a non-food online business in the first half of 2009/10.

Interest in e-commerce within supermarkets is not limited to Sainsbury's. Tesco is one of the world's largest online businesses. Its online grocery sales in 2007 exceeded £1 billion in the UK. It has launched its e-commerce in other countries and has diversified into selling non-grocery items online.

Advantages to a business of e-commerce trading are...

- **24-hour selling** so consumers can shop at any time
- **low cost** to set up and to operate – tills do not need staffing, and overheads such as rent are lower or non-existent
- **trading in new markets** – online sites are national and international
- **communication** is improved, e.g. through email addresses.

The problems of e-commerce include...

- **lack of trust** by consumers when buying over the Internet
- **lack of access to the technology** in some areas and countries
- **lack of language skill** – some customers will not understand English
- **lack of awareness** that the e-commerce site exists.

> **KEY POINT**
>
> Worldwide access to e-commerce outlets varies greatly.

> **PROGRESS CHECK**
>
> 1. State two factors that influence the choice of distribution channel.
> 2. What are two advantages to a retailer of having an e-commerce site?
>
> 1. Cost of the channel; the amount of control over distribution the producer requires.
> 2. **Any two from:** 24-hour selling; new markets can easily be entered, trade in new markets, improved communication.

4.6 Customers and customer service

LEARNING SUMMARY	After studying this section you should be able to understand:
	• the range of customer needs
	• how customer satisfaction can be measured
	• the features and importance of effective customer service

Needs, satisfaction and service

AQA BS	✓
AQA BCS	✗
EDEXCEL BS	✓
EDEXCEL BC	✓
OCR BS	✓
OCR BCS	✓
WJEC BS	✓
CCEA BS	✓

Customer needs

If four different customers go food shopping, we could find that one customer wants the lowest possible price, the second wants a wide choice of foodstuffs, the third customer only looks for the best quality food and the fourth will only buy organically produced food. Different customers therefore have different needs. The main needs are...

A business must discover who its customers are and why they buy its products.

- discovering a product's **value**
- obtaining **information** about a product and its functions
- finding out about **after-sales services**.

Customer needs change according to **customer characteristics**, such as their age and sex, income, location and lifestyle. **Customer satisfaction** will be measured using primary and secondary research methods.

Customer needs:
value for money

Market research takes into consideration customer needs, characteristics and satisfaction, so the business can produce products that its customers want.

A satisfied customer

Customer service

All businesses want **repeat custom**. Customers returning to buy the same product means that the business has established **customer loyalty**, so it holds or increases its market share, improves its image, and has a regular income from sales. Those customers who do not repeat the purchase are likely to have bought from, and moved to, a competing product.

One way to encourage repeat custom is by offering **efficient customer service**. Efficient customer service means that orders are fulfilled correctly and any complaints are dealt with appropriately. Efficient customer service needs efficient...

- **employees** – knowledgeable and helpful with good communication skills
- **delivery** – available products that are delivered when agreed
- **after-sales service** – exchange goods if necessary; the offer of a guarantee
- **location** – for example, a suitable layout, easily to find with parking and other facilities.

> Email is an important recent development to help businesses establish efficient customer service.

Effective customer service

KEY POINT

A business may change its level of customer service according to its target market.

PROGRESS CHECK

1. Give one example of a customer need.
2. State how an employee can help make customer service efficient.

2. Being helpful and communicating effectively
1. Any one from: The need to discover information about a product, the need to discover a product's value, the need to find out about after-sales service.

Sample GCSE questions

This question is based on elements of the marketing mix.

MyMouse Ltd makes plastic casings and mouse mats for computer 'mice'. The company has the technology to start making personalised mouse mats – photos sent to the factory are copied onto mouse mats. Although these mouse mats will be expensive to make, they have proved popular with the company's staff and the directors do not know of any competitors in this area. The directors have a number of outlets they plan to use for the new mouse mats:

- Their own small factory shop, where they sell mouse mats and casings to visitors.
- A small chain of computer shops, which currently sells their existing products.
- the Internet.

(a) What pricing strategy would be appropriate for the new mouse mats?

I think the pricing strategy should be penetration type. This is because MyMouse needs to capture a large market share if it is to sell its new mouse mats **(6)**

(b) Suggest how the directors might make customers aware of this new line.

MyMouse needs to advertise. I wouldn't recommend TV because it's expensive, although at Christmas people do advertise presents like personal mouse mats on TV. There are other ways like cinema advertising but I think something local such as a local paper is best. This would be quite cheap and it is local, where MyMouse is. **(6)**

(c) Evaluate the suitability of each of the proposed outlets for the new mouse mats.

Their own shop is a good idea, because people can bring along their photos and they can do it there and then. It is easy for the company because they don't have to send their mouse mats anywhere, they can get it done there. I recommend the computer shop's outlet because they already deal with them. Will they get as much profit? The shop owners will want money for selling these mats, unlike the factory shop which belongs to MyMouse. The Internet is a great idea, because MyMouse mats are for computers, which we need for the Internet. It means people all over the world can get these mats though they will still have to send a photo or maybe send it electronically? The catch is the Internet is so massive now that not everyone will find out about MyMouse and its mats. **(12)**

A limited answer. 'Penetration' should be described in detail. A better answer would refer to the unique nature of the product – so 'skimming' or 'maximising' may be more appropriate.

Good reference to the local market; linking the advertising medium to the product. Suitable reference to Christmas. This should be developed by relating it to advertising media. The answer could mention likely outlets such as the Internet, and consider promotion such as specialist computer magazines (national).

A good point about visiting, which means the company deals directly with the customer (helps record-keeping, gives personal contact, less expensive). You need to compare strengths and weaknesses of each outlet.

Make points about (i) location of shops (e.g. transport costs); (ii) whether they can create product onsite or must communicate with MyMouse (time and expense).

Mention instructions given and orders made via Internet, MyMouse can display other products, 24-hour sales and direct contact via email, and a cheap medium.

Exam practice questions

The first two questions are on a marketing department and the research it might do.

1 Which of the following illustrate the work of a typical marketing department? **(3)**

A Carrying out market research		**B** Production planning	
C Paying suppliers		**D** Constructing accounts	
E Quality assurance		**F** Using advertising agencies	
G Selecting new staff		**H** Storing raw materials	
I Promoting sales		**J** Ordering new machinery	

2 Which of the following are **secondary** research methods?

    A   Reading trade magazines ☐   **B**   Interviewing customers ☐

    C   Studying Government statistics ☐   **D**   Carrying out surveys ☐

    E   Using telephone polls ☐   **F**   Carrying out opinion polls ☐   **(2)**

3 This question is based on the marketing mix.

SupaSlice Ltd is a company producing a wide range of bread products for the mass market, and cakes for special occasions such as weddings and 18th birthday parties. It sells most of its mass market products through its own chain of shops in the Midlands, and the rest direct to catering establishments in this area. The company adds a percentage to its cost of manufacture to determine the price of these items, though some are sold as loss leaders. It uses a skimming pricing policy for its speciality products, which are promoted – with the company's bread products – through both point-of-sale advertising and advertisements in local papers.

(a) Describe *SupaSlice's* marketing mix.

    ....

    .... **(4)**

(b) Explain the **three** terms underlined in the data.

    ....

    .... **(6)**

(c) Explain the difference in the company's approach to pricing its two types of product.

    ....

    ....

    .... **(6)**

(d) Suggest **two** appropriate forms of market research for *SupaSlice* to use.

    ....

    .... **(4)**

5 Finance in business

The following topics are covered in this chapter:

- The need for finance
- Costs in business
- Financial forecasts
- Financial accounting
- Interpreting accounts

5.1 The need for finance

LEARNING SUMMARY

After studying this section you should be able to understand:

- why businesses need finance
- the main types of internal and external finance available
- limited company shares and debentures
- factors that influence the choice of finance

Why businesses need finance

AQA BS	✓
AQA BCS	✗
EDEXCEL BS	✓
EDEXCEL BC	✓
OCR BS	✓
OCR BCS	✗
WJEC BS	✓
CCEA BS	✓

Entrepreneurs – the business decision makers – need money to start their business. They have to buy or hire the assets (page 97) they will need to make or supply their goods and services.

Once it has been set up, the business must meet its short-term debts that come from trading activities such as buying stock on credit. This short-term finance is known as working capital (page 95). Any business without sufficient working capital will find it difficult to survive. The effects could be that: it cannot take advantage of cost-saving discounts because it doesn't have the cash available; its creditors (suppliers on credit) will demand payment of the money owed to them, and can even take legal action and force the business to close down, selling off its assets to meet the business's debts.

Businesses also need long-term capital so that they can expand. There are many sources of long-term capital: personal savings for sole traders and shares in limited companies are two well-known examples.

> **KEY POINT**
>
> All private and public sector businesses need finance to start, survive and grow.

Sources of finance for the private sector

The most common private sector business organisations – sole traders, partnerships and limited companies – use both internal and external sources of finance. These businesses raise **internal finance** funds by...

- **retained profits** – some profits are kept to develop the business, not withdrawn and spent by the sole traders / partners or distributed as shareholders' dividends
- **selling surplus assets** that are no longer required
- **using trade credit** – the owners may use credit offered to them by their suppliers, and also reduce the credit periods they offer to customers to get more money in quickly
- **investing surplus cash** – the interest on this investment being a source of finance
- **reducing stocks held** so that cash is released and not 'tied up' in these stocks.

Figure 5.1 A trade credit document (an invoice)

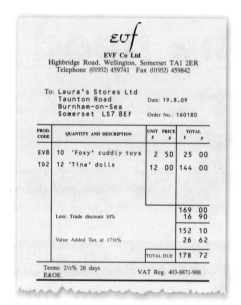

The largest amounts of finance for private sector businesses usually come from **external** sources, which are often long-term:

- **Personal savings** of the sole traders and partners and borrowing from their family and friends.
- **Issuing shares** – the main source for most limited companies, or using **venture capital** (page 85).
- **Loans and mortgages** from banks, building societies and other financial organisations, or from central and local government.
- **Using finance houses** – e.g. leasing (a form of renting) equipment such as photocopiers, or buying assets using credit sale or hire purchase.
- **Overdrafts** from banks – a short-term source where the business arranges with the bank to withdraw more money than there is in its account.
- **Factoring debts** – the business sells its debts to a debt factor company, receiving most of the debt's value immediately rather than having to wait for the full debt to be paid.

KEY POINT

Public sector organisations are funded mainly from taxes, borrowing, or profits made from their trading activities.

Shares and debentures

The most important source of long-term finance for limited companies is through the issue of shares and debentures.

Shares

Holders of **shares** own the company. A public limited company (plc: page 49) is allowed to sell its shares to the general public by issuing a prospectus. Afterwards, its 'second-hand' shares are traded on the Stock Exchange. A private limited company ('ltd': page 49) must sell its shares privately: these cannot be bought and sold on the Stock Exchange.

> Ordinary shares are also called 'equities'.

Ordinary shares allow their holders a **vote** at company meetings. The rate of **dividend** (payment of profits made to the shareholders) depends on the amount of profits: it is a **variable rate**. Ordinary shareholders are the **last to be paid** out of profit and so they face the risk of not receiving any dividend if profits are low. They are also the **last to have their capital repaid** if the company is 'wound up'.

Preference shares do not normally give the right to vote. These shareholders receive priority over ordinary shareholders for paying dividend and repaying capital. The preference dividend is **fixed**. Some preference shares are **cumulative**: if profits in one year are too low to pay the dividend, the amount owing is carried forward to future years and will be paid when future profits are high enough.

Figure 5.2 Ordinary and preference shares

	Ordinary	Preference
Voting rights?	Normally one vote per share	Usually non-voting
Dividend payment?	Variable (high or low depending on profits)	Fixed, regardless of profit level
Capital repaid?	Paid after preference; repaid last	Paid before ordinary; repaid before ordinary

> VC is often used where there is a 'management buy-out' (MBO) or 'buy-in' (MBI), where the managers invest in the business.

Some small and growing companies that want to finance further expansion, but cannot issue more shares or raise the finance by other means, use **venture capital** (VC). This is also known as **private equity** and is provided by specialist VC businesses in return for a proportion of a company's shares. The VC business often requires a say in decision-making by having a representative on the borrowing company's Board of Directors.

> **KEY POINT**
>
> Ordinary shares are more common than preference, and are normally assumed to be the ones meant when 'shares' are being discussed.

Debentures

> 'Debenture' is the name of the document issued to the lenders of this loan.

Debentures are **long-term loans** (often called 'loan stock'). The debenture holders are **creditors** of the company, not the owners (unlike shareholders). The loan will normally be **secured** against the assets of the company: if the company cannot repay the loan, the debenture holder has the right to sell the asset to recover the debt owed. In return for this loan the debenture holder receives **interest**, which must be paid by the company whether it is making a profit or a loss. Like other loans, a **debenture loan will be repaid** in the future.

Figure 5.3 Shareholders and debenture holders

	Shareholders	Debenture Holders
Status?	Owners of the company	Lenders to the company
Reward?	Dividend, paid out of business expense	Interest, paid whether or not the company makes a profit
Repayment?	Not normally repaid, unless the company is wound up	Normally repayable at a future date: if company is wound up; repaid before shareholders

> **KEY POINT**
>
> Debenture interest is a normal business expense, and not paid out of the company's net profits.

Selecting the source of finance

AQA BS	✓
AQA BCS	✗
EDEXCEL BS	✓
EDEXCEL BC	✓
OCR BS	✓
OCR BCS	✗
WJEC BS	✓
CCEA BS	✓

Businesses do not normally rely on one source of finance, and there is usually a range of short-term and long-term sources from which they can choose. The main factors influencing which source is chosen are shown in Figure 5.4 below.

Figure 5.4 Factors influencing the source of finance chosen

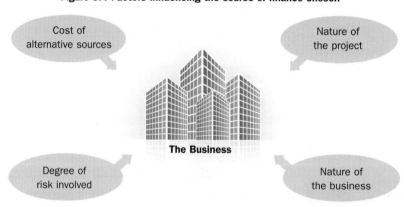

The main **start-up sources** of finance include loans, personal savings, and share capital. These are also popular sources of **finance for growth**: others include overdrafts and venture capital.

Firms often need extra finance for projects such as launching a new product. The **nature of the project** influences the source of finance. For example, businesses with projects requiring a lot of 'high-tech' equipment may choose to lease (rather than buy) items to ensure they keep using the most up-to-date equipment.

The **nature of the business** also influences the source of finance. Some sources are only available to certain forms of business ownership. Firms in high-risk areas, and smaller firms, may find their sources of finance are restricted and that the cost of finance (the rate of interest charged) is higher than average.

> Shares illustrate a source of finance only available to a certain form of ownership (limited company).

> **KEY POINT**
>
> The finance chosen will depend on whether the business is **starting up** or seeking to **expand**, and whether it wants **short-term** or **long-term** finance.

5.2 Costs in business

LEARNING SUMMARY	After studying this section you should be able to understand:
	• how costs are classified
	• the difference between...
	– fixed, variable and semi-variable costs
	– direct and indirect costs
	– average and marginal costs

Costs of production

AQA BS	✓
AQA BCS	✗
EDEXCEL BS	✓
EDEXCEL BC	✓
OCR BS	✓
OCR BCS	✗
WJEC BS	✓
CCEA BS	✓

Although efficient, large-scale production can create **economies of scale** (pages 128–129) which help to reduce costs, a business still has to meet the various costs of production. Businesses group these costs under different headings to help **analyse** and **control** them. Figure 5.5 illustrates the typical costs to a business.

Figure 5.5 Typical costs of production

The different types of cost apply not only to production ('factory' costs), but also to administration and to the selling and distribution ('office' costs).

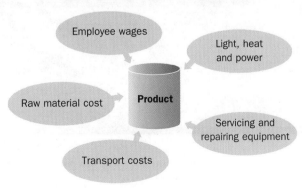

Fixed and variable costs

We can separate the different costs of a business into those that are fixed and those that are variable:

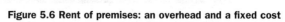

- **Fixed costs do not change as output changes.** Examples include factory and office rent, office salaries (these do not depend on the number of items produced) and insurance premiums, e.g. for business vehicles. These costs will not change whether the factory is working at 100% capacity or whether it is closed.
- **Variable costs change as output changes.** These costs arise from a business's production activities, and therefore change as the output level changes. Examples include the costs of raw materials used to make the products, and 'piece-work' wages where employees are paid by the number of items they make.

An important reason for analysing costs as fixed and variable is for 'break-even analysis' (page 89).

In reality, the distinction between fixed and variable is not always easy to make. Many costs are **semi-variable**, containing elements that are fixed and variable. For example, a factory's power costs may carry a fixed 'standing charge' element that must be paid whether or not any power is used, and a (variable) charge per unit of power used.

> **KEY POINT**
>
> Fixed costs will change over time – insurance premiums go up, staff salaries rise, factory rent increases – but they do not change in the short-term as output changes.

Direct and indirect costs

A business's **direct costs** are those that can be **directly linked to particular product lines**. Examples include the costs of running the machinery used to manufacture individual products, and the cost of raw materials used in the product.

Direct costs are normally variable, and indirect costs are normally fixed.

Indirect costs are also known as **overheads**. These are shared between the different product lines and **do not relate to one particular product line**. Examples include the cost of stationery used for all the company's products and services, salaries of office staff who are involved with all the products, and the office and factory rent. Managers want to know the cost of making individual products to calculate their profitability so decisions can be made (e.g. about prices). An accountant will therefore **apportion** (share out) the indirect costs to the different product lines, e.g. sharing factory rent on the amount of floor space used by each product line.

Figure 5.6 Rent of premises: an overhead and a fixed cost

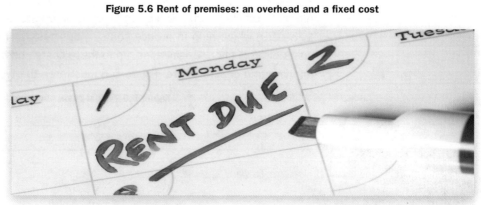

> **KEY POINT**
>
> The **total costs** for a business consist of **fixed plus variable** costs; they also consist of **direct plus indirect** costs.

Average and marginal costs

Economies of scale create lower unit costs (cost per item made). This **average cost of production** is found by dividing total output by total cost. The **marginal cost** of a product is the **cost of making that individual product**. The marginal cost will not normally be the same as the product's average cost because of the way fixed costs are distributed.

For example, if total fixed costs are £3 000 and variable costs are £100 per item made:

- average cost of making one item = $\frac{£3\,100}{1}$ = £3 100
- average cost of making two items = $\frac{£3\,200}{2}$ = £1 600
- average cost to make three items = $\frac{£3\,300}{3}$ = £1 100.

The marginal cost of the second and third items is, however, only £100.

> **KEY POINT**
>
> Managers find this information helpful, e.g. when deciding whether to take on a new order and what price to charge for it.

> **PROGRESS CHECK**
>
> 1. State the difference between:
>   (a) direct and indirect costs;
>   (b) fixed and variable costs.
> 2. Give one example of:
>   (a) a fixed cost;
>   (b) a variable cost.
>
> 1. (a) Direct costs are directly linked to product lines; indirect costs are more general (overheads).
>   (b) Fixed costs do not change with output; variable costs do.
> 2. (a) **Any suitable answers**, e.g. factory or office rent;
>   (b) **Any suitable answers**, e.g. the raw materials used in a product.

5.3 Financial forecasts

LEARNING SUMMARY	**After studying this section you should be able to understand:**
	- the nature and importance of break-even analysis
	- how to construct and interpret break-even information
	- the nature of standard costing and business budgets
	- cash budgeting and forecasting

Break-even analysis

AQA BS	✓
AQA BCS	✗
EDEXCEL BS	✓
EDEXCEL BC	✓
OCR BS	✓
OCR BCS	✗
WJEC BS	✓
CCEA BS	✓

Break-even analysis calculates at what point the business 'breaks even': the point at which it is making **neither a profit nor a loss**. The break-even point for a business is therefore where **total costs equal total revenues**. This point (of output) is important to a business because it is beyond this point that the business starts to make a profit.

Break-even analysis uses **fixed and variable costs** to calculate the break-even point and to show it on a graph.

Constructing the break-even chart

To construct the chart (or graph) we need information on fixed costs, variable costs and selling price. We then plot the results on a graph that has £ (costs and revenue) on the vertical (*y*) axis, and production/output (number made and sold) on the horizontal (*x*) axis.

For example, assume that a company is making a product. The selling price is £3, fixed costs are £10 000, variable costs are 50p per item, and 5 000 products will be made and sold:

- **Fixed cost** (**FC**) **line**. The fixed cost line is plotted as a straight line that starts at the £10 000 point on the vertical axis and runs parallel to the horizontal axis (because fixed costs stay constant at £10 000). Figure 5.7, below, shows this break-even chart with the fixed cost line labelled.
- **Variable cost** (**VC**). If output is 5 000, total variable costs are £2 500 (5 000 × 50p).
- **Total cost** (**TC**) **line**. Total costs = fixed costs + variable costs. We plot the total cost line on the chart starting at where the fixed cost line meets the vertical axis: at this (zero) output there are no variable costs so total cost = fixed cost. At the other end of the line (the 5 000 output point) the gap between total costs and fixed costs is £2 500 (that is, the total variable costs at this output). Total costs at output of 5 000 units are £12 500, i.e. £10 000 FC + £2 500 VC. The total cost line can now be drawn between the two output figures (zero and 5 000) as shown in Figure 5.7.
- **Total revenue** (**TR**) **line**. The TR line can be plotted. The selling price is £3 so the total revenue at the maximum output will be £15 000 (£3 × 5 000). We can draw the TR line by joining this point on the graph to the zero point where the two axes meet (because at an output of zero, revenue is also zero).
- **Break-even point**. The firm's break-even point is where the **TR and TC lines cross**. A line drawn from this point down to the Output axis shows that 4 000 units represents the **break-even level of output**. Selling over 4 000 units will give a profit: the triangle below it, representing sales and output under 4 000, is the area of loss.
- **Margin of safety**. If 5 000 units are sold, the margin of safety is between 5 000 and the break-even point: the business knows that its sales can fall by 1 000 (the margin of safety) to 4 000 before it starts to make a loss.

> Remember examples of fixed costs (e.g. rent) and variable costs (e.g. raw materials).

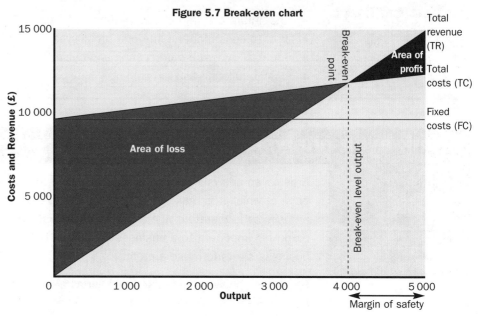

Figure 5.7 Break-even chart

The profit or loss at all levels of output can be read from the chart. For example, at output and sales of 4 500, the TR line shows £13 500 and the TC line reads £12 250. The gap between these two lines – the profit, since TR is above TC – is £1 250.

Calculating the break-even point

Managers are interested in the amount of contribution a product makes to its fixed costs. These fixed costs must be met, regardless of whatever level of output the business is making and selling. Calculate the contribution that each product makes towards meeting the fixed costs by:

Selling price – Variable cost = Contribution

When enough individual contributions have been made, the business's fixed costs will be covered (paid): this is its break-even point.

In our example, selling price is £3 and variable cost 50p. The contribution is:

£3.00 – 50p = £2.50

Each item sold contributes £2.50 towards the £10 000 fixed costs. Calculate the break-even point by dividing the unit contribution into total fixed costs. This shows that 4 000 is, as we have seen from the chart, the break-even point.

$$\frac{\textbf{Total fixed costs}}{\textbf{Unit contribution}} = \frac{\textbf{£10 000}}{\textbf{£2.50}} = \textbf{4 000}$$

Check the chart on page 90 to prove the company is losing £2 500 at an output of 3 000 units.

The profit or loss at each level of production / sales can also be calculated. For example, sales of 3 000 give a total contribution of £7 500 (3 000 × £2.50). The fixed costs are still £10 000, so at this level of sales the company would be making a loss of £2 500.

The usefulness of break-even analysis

Break-even analysis provides information about how many items a business must sell at a certain price before making a profit. The effect of **changing figures**, such as the price, can be assessed through the effect on the break-even point and margin of safety.

Break-even analysis does have limitations. Its information might be inaccurate or out-of-date because it analyses the situation at a particular time only. It is of limited use for service industries that do not make products, and for multi-product businesses, because it becomes difficult to calculate the various costs for individual products. It also assumes...

- all output is sold, and sold at the same price – this is often not so, for example, all the output may not be sold and a business might lower the product price to sell more of them
- variable costs per unit stay constant – in practice cost may fall, for example, through economies of scale such as bulk buying
- fixed costs stay fixed – they are fixed only within a certain output, for example, if another building is rented when output grows, this increases the fixed costs.

> **KEY POINT**
>
> Beyond the break-even output, a profit is made; before it, a loss is made.

Cash budgets and forecasts

AQA BS	✓
AQA BCS	✗
EDEXCEL BS	✓
EDEXCEL BC	✓
OCR BS	✓
OCR BCS	✗
WJEC BS	✓
CCEA BS	✓

All organisations need sufficient working capital (page 95) to meet debts due for payment. Businesses forecast working capital and a key element in this is **forecasting cash flows**. Forecasting cash movement is illustrated in Figure 5.8.

Figure 5.8 Movement of cash

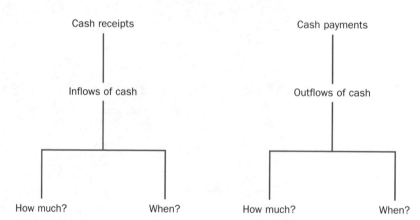

By preparing forecasts of cash coming in and going out of the business the accountant can identify times of the year when there will be **shortfalls**. This means that, for example, an overdraft can be arranged with the bank. **Surpluses** of cash will also be shown, which can be invested by the firm on a short-term basis.

Below is the layout of a typical cash forecast. It shows the expected future cash movements so that managers can see the effects of their plans on the business's cash flow.

Figure 5.9 A cash forecast

Cash forecast	January £000	February £000	March £000
INFLOWS			
Sales	450	420	470
Other Income	50	30	40
TOTAL INFLOWS	500	450	510
OUTFLOWS			
Raw Materials	60	80	110
Wages	80	80	90
Selling Expenses	10	20	25
Rent and Rates	5	5	5
Light and Heat	5	5	5
Buying Assets		300	50
Other Outflows	25	10	30
TOTAL OUTFLOWS	185	500	315
NET CASH SURPLUS OR DEFICIT	315	(50)	195
BALANCE FROM LAST MONTH	25	340	290
BALANCE TO CARRY FORWARD	340	290	485

KEY POINT

Companies that publish their accounts must show cash movements in their business over the last year.

PROGRESS CHECK

1 Define the term 'break-even point'.
2 How is the break-even point calculated?
3 Why is it important to forecast future cash flows?

1. The break-even point is where neither a profit nor a loss is being made.
2. It is calculated by dividing total fixed costs by the unit contribution.
3. To ensure that expected shortfalls can be covered, e.g. by overdrafts, and that surpluses can be acted upon, e.g. by short-term investment.

5.4 Financial accounting

LEARNING SUMMARY

After studying this section you should be able to understand:

- why financial accounting is important in business
- what 'profitability' and 'liquidity' mean
- the main financial statements:
  - the profit and loss account
  - the balance sheet

The purposes of financial accounting

AQA BS	✓
AQA BCS	✗
EDEXCEL BS	✓
EDEXCEL BC	✗
OCR BS	✓
OCR BCS	✗
WJEC BS	✓
CCEA BS	✓

Obtaining information

The accounts department get information from sources such as...

- copies of sales invoices – from which the value of sales can be calculated
- cheques from debtors – which will be banked
- statements from creditors – which will have to be paid.

Recording information

Information is recorded in the accounts; this is the **book-keeping** role of financial accounting.

Analysing information

Once the financial transactions are recorded the accountant can analyse this information, by calculating **accounting ratios** (page 98–101), to highlight financial trends. Some 'advance planning', such as **budgeting** (page 92), can be carried out once financial information is recorded and analysed.

Presenting information

The accountant has a key role as a communicator of financial information. The accountant must present it to the rest of the management team and the various stakeholder groups who are interested in this financial information:

Figure 5.10 The groups who are interested in financial information

Profitability and liquidity

> Profit is both a reward for risk-taking and an internal source of funds for the business.

One reason for keeping accounts is to record the business **revenues** (income) and **expenses**, from which profit is calculated. The amount of profit can be compared against other important figures, especially the value of sales made and the value of the capital employed in the business. This gives a guide to business **profitability**.

> **KEY POINT**
>
> 'Profitability' and 'profit' are related but different: profitability is a judgement on whether the amount of profit is adequate.

A business's **liquidity** refers to its **ability to meet debts as they fall due**. A business will have both **current assets** (cash and 'near-cash' items such as its stock, and money owed by its debtors), and **current liabilities** (its own short-term debts, such as the money it owes to suppliers). The difference between these totals is its **working capital**, also known as **net current assets**.

Figure 5.11 A company's working capital

		£000	£000
Current assets			
	Stock		250
	Debtors		490
	Cash in Hand		10
			750
Current liabilities			
	Creditors	370	
	Bank Overdraft	30	
			400
Working capital			350

The amount of working capital is important because it shows **whether the business is able to pay its debts**. If, for example, its current assets are £30 000 and its current liabilities are £20 000, the business has enough cash and 'near-cash' to meet its £20 000 debts due shortly. If, however, it had £20 000 current assets and £30 000 current liabilities, the business would struggle to find enough money to pay its debts.

> **KEY POINT**
>
> In the short term, liquidity is far more important to a business than profitability.

Financial statements

AQA BS	✓
AQA BCS	✗
EDEXCEL BS	✓
EDEXCEL BC	✗
OCR BS	✓
OCR BCS	✗
WJEC BS	✓
CCEA BS	✓

A business will produce a set of 'final accounts':

● Its **profit and loss account** calculates net profit.

● Its **balance sheet** displays assets and liabilities – what it owns and what it owes.

The profit and loss account

The profit and loss account will contain a section, sometimes referred to as a separate account, showing the firm's **trading** (buying and selling). Its purpose is to calculate **gross profit**: Figure 5.12 below shows that this is the difference between the sales revenue and the cost of these sales.

Figure 5.12 The trading account

N. Merchant Trading account for year ending 31 December	£ (000)	£ (000)
Sales		400
Less cost of sales:		
Opening stock	55	
Purchases	290	
	345	
Closing stock	(45)	
		300
Gross profit		**100**

The profit and loss account calculates the **net profit** – the balance left after all expenses are deducted from gross profit. There will be administration, selling, and distribution expenses. Examples include rent and rates, light and heat, wages and salaries, and...

● **depreciation** – the cost of 'using up' the major assets of the business, e.g. the wear and tear that occurs on furniture, vehicles and machinery

● **bad debts** (the cost of selling on credit) – when a debtor cannot pay the debt owed to the business, it has to write the debtor off as an expense.

Figure 5.13 The profit and loss account

N. Merchant Profit and loss account for year ending 31 December	£ (000)	£ (000)
Gross profit		100
Less expenses:		
Administration	32	
Selling and distribution	16	
Financial	12	
		60
Net profit		**40**

The balance sheet

> Capital expenditure, shown in the balance sheet, does not affect profit calculations.

The purpose of a balance sheet is to show what the business **owns** (assets) and what it **owes** (liabilities). Payment made for its assets is called **capital expenditure**.

Items in the balance sheet often appear under these headings:
- **Fixed assets** – these assets have a long life and are bought to work in the business and not to re-sell.
- **Current assets** – these assets (stocks, debtors, bank and cash) change regularly in amount and are linked to trading.
- **Current liabilities** – these are short-term debts for the business and are often shown as deductions from current assets in order to give the working capital figure (also known as **net current assets**). Current liabilities of limited companies include **proposed dividends** (owed to shareholders) and **corporation tax** (owed to the government).
- **Capital** – this is the owners' investment in the business and is a liability because it is owed to the owners. **Share capital** is shown for companies by its **reserves**, which include undistributed profits, and **loan capital** such as debentures.

Figure 5.14 The balance sheet

N.Merchant   Balance sheet as at 31 December

	£ (000) Cost	£ (000) Depreciation	£ (000) Net
Fixed assets			
Land and buildings	100	—	100
Plant and equipment	24	6	18
Vehicles	5	3	2
	129	9	120
Current assets			
Stocks		45	
Debtors		25	
Bank and cash		20	
		90	
Current liabilities			
Creditors	20		
Accrued expenses	10		
		30	
Net current assets			60
Net assets			180
Capital			
Opening balance			140
Net profit for year			40
			180

KEY POINT

The profit and loss account shows the business's **financial performance**; the balance sheet shows its **financial position**.

PROGRESS CHECK

1. What does the accounting function do with financial information?
2. State the difference between profitability and liquidity.

1. Obtain; record; analyse; present.
2. Profitability measures profit against turnover/capital; liquidity assesses the ability to pay debts as they become due for payment.

5.5 Interpreting accounts

LEARNING SUMMARY	**After studying this section you should be able to understand:** ● what the main profitability, liquidity and efficiency ratios are ● how they are calculated ● what the results of these calculations tell you

Areas of analysis

AQA BS	✓
AQA BCS	✗
EDEXCEL BS	✓
EDEXCEL BC	✗
OCR BS	✓
OCR BCS	✗
WJEC BS	✓
CCEA BS	✓

Profitability, liquidity and efficiency are the three main areas for analysis.

Profitability ratios

> Remember that 'turnover' is another name for Sales.

Name	Calculation	Purpose
Gross Profit Margin (%)	$\dfrac{\text{Gross Profit}}{\text{Turnover}} \times 100$	To show what percentage of turnover is represented by gross profit (how many pence out of every £1 sales is gross profit)

If this percentage is increasing, the business is receiving more gross profit for every £1 sales. If falling, the business's profit margin is smaller than before (e.g. it has cut its selling price, or costs of sales are more expensive).

Name	Calculation	Purpose
Net Profit Margin (%)	$\dfrac{\text{Net Profit}}{\text{Turnover}} \times 100$	To show what percentage of turnover is represented by net profit (how many pence out of every £1 sales is net profit).

An increase in this percentage means the business is making a higher net profit per £1 of sales than before. This may be due to a change in the gross profit %, or perhaps the business's expenses as a percentage of sales have fallen.

Name	Calculation	Purpose
Return on Capital Employed (ROCE)	$\dfrac{\text{Net Profit}}{\text{Capital Employed}} \times 100$	To show how profitable the owners' investment is by calculating the percentage return.

This figure – how many pence net profit for every £1 capital employed – can be compared to the rate of return the owners would like to receive if they invested elsewhere. This indicates to them whether it is worthwhile continuing to invest in the business.

Liquidity ratios

Name	Calculation	Purpose
Working Capital Ratio ('Current Ratio')	Current Assets to Current Liabilities (as a ratio)	To check the ability of the business to pay its short-term debts
Liquid Capital ('Acid Test') Ratio	Current Assets less Stock, to Current Liabilities (as a ratio)	To see if the business can meet its short-term debts without having to sell any stock

Asset efficiency ratios

Average Stock is calculated by totalling the opening and closing stocks, and dividing by 2.

Name	Calculation	Purpose
Rate of Stock Turnover ('Stockturn')	$\dfrac{\text{Cost of Sales}}{\text{Average Stock}}$	To give the number of times per period that the average stock is sold

If the stockturn is increasing, it's likely that the business is holding lower average stocks than before and is operating more efficiently, and vice versa.

Name	Calculation	Purpose
Debtors' Collection Period ('Debtor days')	$\dfrac{\text{Debtors}}{\text{Turnover}} \times 365$	To show the length of time (number of days) on average that it takes debtors to pay their debts to the business

Name	Calculation	Purpose
Creditors' Collection Period	$\dfrac{\text{Creditors}}{\text{Purchases}} \times 365$	To show the length of time (number of days) on average that the business takes to pay its creditors

The debtors' collection period shows how efficient the business is at collecting its debts: it is being more efficient if the number of days is falling, and vice versa. With the creditors' collection period, an increase means that the business is taking a longer credit period, either because it is better at getting credit or because it is facing problems in paying its creditors.

Using ratios

Study the following final accounts. We can use these figures to calculate ratios.

Figure 5.15 Final accounts

TRADING and PROFIT and LOSS ACCOUNTS
for the Year Ended 31 December

	£000	£000
Turnover		1 000
less: cost of Sales:		
Opening Stock	40	
Purchases	620	
	660	
Closing Stock	60	
		600
Gross Profit		400
less: expenses:		
Rent and Rates	20	
Light and Heat	10	
Advertising	25	
Wages and Salaries	70	
Office Expenses	125	
Depreciation	45	
Bad Debts	5	
		300
Net Profit		100

BALANCE SHEET as at 31 December

	£000	£000	£000
FIXED ASSETS			
Premises			200
Machinery			60
Vehicles			40
			300
CURRENT ASSETS			
Closing Stock		60	
Debtors		100	
Cash at Bank		20	
		180	
CURRENT LIABILITIES			
Creditors	60		
Proposed Dividend	20		
Unpaid Corporation Tax	40	120	
NET CURRENT ASSETS			60
NET ASSETS			360
Financed by:			
SHARE CAPITAL			
200 000 £1 Ordinary Shares			200
RESERVES			
General Reserve		70	
Undistributed Profits		30	100
LOAN CAPITAL			
Debentures			60
			360

Using the figures from these final accounts, the ratios are:

- **Gross profit margin** $\dfrac{400}{1\,000} \times 100 = 40\%$

Gross profit is 40p for every £1 of sales (therefore the remaining 60p in the £1 represents the business's cost of sales).

- **Net profit margin** $\dfrac{100}{1\,000} \times 100 = 10\%$

Every £1 of sales gives 10p net profit: the difference between the 40p gross profit and 10p net profit represents the expenses (30p in every £1 of sales).

- **Return on capital employed** $\dfrac{100}{300} \times 100 = 33.3\%$

Every £1 of capital employed (here the capital invested plus reserves figures are used) in the business earns over 33p profit for the shareholders.

> Remember that 'Acid Test' is another name for Liquid Assets.

- **Working capital ratio** $180 : 120 = 3 : 2$ ($1\frac{1}{2} : 1$) current assets to current liabilities. The business has £1.50 'near cash' to pay every £1 of its short-term debts.
- **Liquid assets ratio** (180 – 60 stock gives) $120 : 120$, or $1 : 1$ liquid assets to current liabilities. The business can meet short-term debts without selling any stock.
- **Rate of stock turnover** $\dfrac{600}{50} = 12$ times a year

The business takes a month, on average, to 'turn over' (buy and sell) its stock.

- **Debtors' collection period** $\dfrac{100}{1\,000} \times 365 = 36.5$ days

Debtors take, on average, just over 5 weeks to pay their debts owed to the business.

- **Creditors' collection period** $\dfrac{60}{600} \times 365 = 36.5$ days

The business also takes, on average, 36.5 days' credit from its suppliers.

KEY POINT

Ratios are no use on their own: we must compare this year's ratios to previous ones to see **trends**, and to those of its competitors to check **competitiveness**.

PROGRESS CHECK

1. Name two...
   (a) profitability ratios
   (b) liquidity ratios
   (c) efficiency ratios.
2. What is the item that is included in the Current Ratio but not in the Acid Test?

2. Stock
(c) **Any two from:** Stockturn, debtor days, creditors' collection period.
(b) Current ratio, liquid capital ratio
1. (a) **Any two from:** Net profit margin, ROCE, gross profit margin

Sample GCSE questions

Below is a summary from *Hill Ltd's* financial statements for 2009 and 2008.

	2009 £	2008 £
Sales	4 243 840	4 149 242
Expenses	3 757 848	4 036 570
Fixed assets	551 666	262 124
Current assets	1 804 880	1 645 938
Current liabilities	732 826	689 824
Capital and reserves	1 623 720	1 218 238

(a) Name two likely expenses for *Hill Ltd*.

Rent; machinery; wages. **(2)**

> Two are correct but 'machinery' is a fixed asset, not an expense. 'Machine repairs' or 'machine depreciation' would be correct since they are expenses.

(b) Give another name for Sales.

Another name is Gross Profit. **(1)**

> This is wrong: 'turnover' is the other name.

(c) Identify which item in the financial statements above shows equipment.

Current assets. **(1)**

> Incorrect: equipment is a fixed asset.

(d) Identify which item in the financial statements above shows stocks.

Current assets. **(1)**

> Correct

(e) (i) Calculate the amount of *Hill Ltd's* working capital for both years.

2009 Current assets £1 804 880– current liabilities £732 826 = £1 072 054.
2008 Current assets £1 645 938– current liabilities £689 824 = £956 114. **(4)**

> A good answer: workings are shown (VERY important in figure-work); the method is shown (you can still get marks for a wrong calculation if you show you know HOW to calculate the answer); and the calculations are correct.

(ii) Comment on the change in working capital.

Working capital has increased by over £100 000, which is good. **(2)**

> Correct, but the exact figure could have been given, and 'which is good' on its own is rather vague.

Sample GCSE questions

(iii) What difficulties will *Hill Ltd* face if it has no working capital?

The main problem the directors would face is that they can't pay debts. This means that Hill Ltd can't pay people like its employees, or its suppliers. If this happens, they won't get materials and be able to make and sell their products. **(4)**

(iv) Calculate one liquidity ratio for both years and comment on your results.

In 2009 the Current Ratio was 1 804 880 / 732 826, which gives 2.46 to 1. In 2008 the Current Ratio was 1 645 938 / 689 824, which gives 2.38 to 1. **(4)**

(f) **(i)** Compare the capital and reserves and the fixed assets figures for both years.

The figures show that both the fixed assets and the capital and reserves have increased. **(4)**

(ii) What are likely reasons for the changes in these amounts?

With fixed assets, more could have been bought because the company is expanding. Capital and reserves increase by either putting more capital in, or keeping some of the profits as reserves. **(4)**

(g) Name two other ratios that should be calculated from the full final accounts of Hill Ltd, and outline the purpose of each ratio.

The Debtors Collection ratio could be calculated, which shows how quickly Hill Ltd collects its debts from selling on credit. The Stock Turnover ratio could be calculated to check how often this company is selling its (average) stock. **(4)**

A good answer, but draw a conclusion: the directors may face going out of business through not being able to meet the business debts.

Correct calculations (Acid Test cannot be calculated because there are no stock figures), but the calculations need supporting by a comment such as 'Hill Ltd's Current Ratio shows an increase, which confirms its liquidity seems sufficient, although we do not know its stock position'.

This is correct, but the amount of the increase should be calculated: £289 542 and £405 482 respectively.

Again, this is a good answer, but it would be improved by giving examples of fixed assets that might have been bought (machinery, equipment), and by stating who will have put more capital in (the shareholders).

A suitable choice of two relevant ratios, supported by an accurate outline of the purpose of each ratio.

Exam practice questions

This question is about break-even analysis.

1 Bill Smith was recently made redundant. Bill decided to use his redundancy money to establish his own business so that he could work from home, something he had always wanted to do. Bill enjoys painting and going to the cinema, and he decided to paint some of his favourite movie stars, and sell them at craft fairs. Bill intends to pay himself a salary of £200 for each fair he attends. He will sell each painting for £30.

For each fair, Bill estimates that his costs will be as follows:

Salary	£200
Rent of a stall	£60
Average travel cost per fair	£40
Production costs per poster	£10

Bill hopes to at least break-even at the start of his new venture.

(a) What does break-even mean?

.... **(1)**

(b) Draw a break-even chart for Bill on the graph below. Label all lines. **(5)**

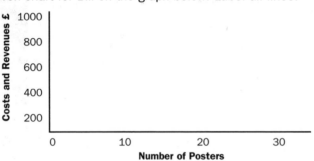

(c) Identify on the graph the number of paintings Bill must sell at each fair to break-even.

.... **(1)**

(d) Bill hopes on average to sell 20 paintings per fair.

What profit or loss will Bill make if he sells 20 paintings at each fair?

.... **(2)**

(e) The director of a large chain of shops met Bill at a fair and has offered to sell Bill's paintings in the shops. Bill knows that a large order could create problems for him.

    (i) What are the main problems that Bill will face if he accepts the offer?

    ....

    .... **(4)**

    (ii) Is Bill likely to be able to overcome these problems? Give reasons for your answer.

    ....

    .... **(4)**

6 People in business

The following topics are covered in this chapter:

- **Human Resources and employing people**
- **Training employees**
- **Remunerating employees**
- **Motivating employees**
- **Protecting employees**

6.1 Human Resources and employing people

LEARNING SUMMARY

After studying this section you should be able to understand:

- the role of the Human Resources (personnel) function
- what a typical Human Resources Department does
- how employees are recruited, selected, appointed and dismissed

Human Resources

AQA BS	✓
AQA BCS	✓
EDEXCEL BS	✓
EDEXCEL BC	✓
OCR BS	✓
OCR BCS	✗
WJEC BS	✓
CCEA BS	✓

The role of the Human Resources (HR) function in business is to deal with people who work, and those wish to work, in an organisation. Larger organisations will have a specialist Human Resources Department.

The work carried out

Below is a summary of the work of Human Resources:

Figure 6.1 The work of Human Resources

Recruitment and selection

Welfare

Wages & salaries

Records

Industrial relations

Training

Voluntary leaving, retirement, redundancy and dismissal

As the business expands or as its employees retire or leave for other jobs, new people have to be recruited. The role of Human Resources in **recruitment** is to inform potential employees that there are vacancies available. Following the advertising of these vacancies, HR Department staff work with their colleagues from the departments with the vacancies to **select** the best applicant for the job.

New employees will be given **training**. All employees benefit from training, so the HR Department also provides training opportunities for existing staff. Human Resources work is also concerned with **staff welfare**. High levels of motivation lead to a happy and contented workforce, which in turn leads to high-quality output being produced. HR staff are involved in ensuring that minimum health, safety and other standards are met, and they may also be asked by employees facing work-related or personal problems to help with these.

Employee details are kept by Human Resources as **staff records**. These details include personal information such as home address, as well as work-related information such as pay rates, training courses attended and promotions received. Since Human Resources deals with employee records, it may also be responsible for calculating and distributing **wages and salaries** and for negotiating and developing the organisation's pay structure. One of its key roles linked to this negotiation is **labour relations** – the HR Department has an important part to play in helping resolve disputes (and in avoiding them in the first place).

Recruiting people

AQA BS	✓
AQA BCS	✓
EDEXCEL BS	✓
EDEXCEL BC	✓
OCR BS	✓
OCR BCS	✗
WJEC BS	✓
CCEA BS	✓

Managers of the department where there is a vacant job position will consider both the **type of work** the position requires and the **type of person** best suited to this work. A **job description** contains details of the type of work and a **person specification** contains information about the type of person best suited to this work.

Information in the job description and person specification will be used to help construct a job advertisement for the vacancy.

The job description	The person specification
Details of the **work**: • job title and location • details of the duties • any special features of the job • any special equipment used	Details of the **person**: • personal qualities • expected qualifications • work experience • physical / mental abilities required

Figure 6.2 Job advertisements

Advertising the vacancy

Job adverts tend to be informative rather than persuasive and are subject to laws that make sure they don't discriminate, for example, in a racist or sexist way.

The firm may advertise internally. Adverts are displayed on noticeboards, sent to employees via email or a printed circular, or published in the business's magazine. Filling the vacancy from existing staff can be quicker and less expensive than recruiting from outside. It also improves morale because existing staff realise that promotion is possible. However, with internal appointments no 'new blood' is introduced, which could lead to fewer new ideas.

If the post is to be advertised externally, HR staff must decide where to advertise. Popular places for the advert are:

- JobCentre Plus. Part of the Department for Work and Pensions, JobCentre Plus is a government agency that offers free vacancy advertising to business people, who can create adverts online, or by email or telephoning them in.

Email and the internet are increasingly used for advertising jobs.

Figure 6.3 JobCentre Plus advertisement

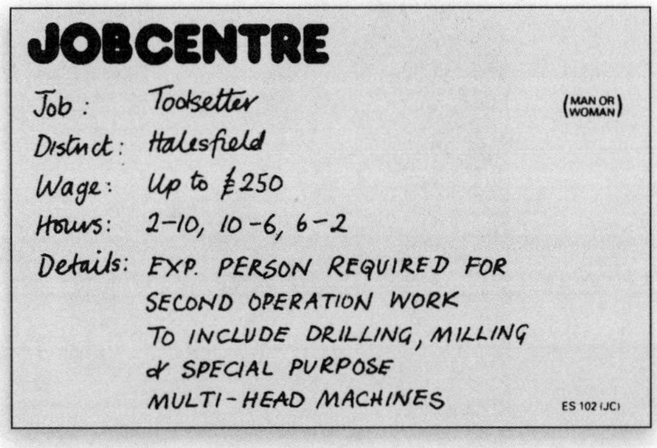

> ## JOBCENTRE
> Job: Toolsetter (MAN OR WOMAN)
> District: Halesfield
> Wage: Up to £250
> Hours: 2–10, 10–6, 6–2
> Details: EXP. PERSON REQUIRED FOR SECOND OPERATION WORK TO INCLUDE DRILLING, MILLING & SPECIAL PURPOSE MULTI-HEAD MACHINES
> ES 102 (JC)

- Recruitment agencies. A business can send details of a vacancy to a local or national agency, such as Pertemps Recruitment, Reed or Brook Street. People seeking work can search the agency's Internet database while agencies can check their own records for people who have registered with them to provide potential staff for interview. The agency receives a fee if the person is appointed, or (often in the case of temporary staff), the business pays the agency, which in turn pays the temporary employee.
- Newspapers and magazines. Many professional and managerial vacancies are advertised in the 'quality' newspapers, or in specialist magazines or journals of the professional bodies. Local papers are also used for managerial, clerical and manual vacancies.

Interested applicants normally have to complete a job application form in which they give details of their education and experience. They are also asked to provide references from people who are prepared to support their application.

As an alternative to sending out a standard application form, the HR Department might ask applicants to submit a curriculum vitae (CV). This CV will contain basically the same information as that asked for on a typical application form.

KEY POINT

All businesses have to recruit people...
- to replace those who have left for another job or have retired, been dismissed or promoted to a new post in the business
- to bring in new skills that are required.

Selecting people

AQA BS	✓
AQA BCS	✓
EDEXCEL BS	✓
EDEXCEL BC	✓
OCR BS	✓
OCR BCS	✗
WJEC BS	✓
CCEA BS	✓

Once applications are received, decisions must be made about the shortlist. This is drawn up by eliminating applicants who do not meet the person specification, for example, they may be too inexperienced or too overqualified. Laws relating to discrimination (page 120) must be observed.

The interview

At an interview the interviewer can discuss information on the application form, and...

- check whether the interviewee's communication skills are up to the required standard
- assess the interviewee's social skills and confidence and check their physical appearance (regarded as important for some jobs, e.g. receptionist)
- judge whether the interviewee will work effectively with colleagues in the department.

> Remember that an interview is a two-way process.

The interviewee can...

- discuss future prospects, such as the possibility of promotion
- check the working conditions and see the facilities available
- ask about training and other opportunities
- judge the friendliness or otherwise of the present staff.

Some organisations run a series of selection tests to help decide which of the short-listed applicants is most suitable for the post. These tests may be designed to assess a candidate's intelligence, personality or aptitude (suitability) for the post. Personal skills such as teamworking, entrepreneurial skills, motivation, communication and supervisory skills can be assessed:

- Intelligence tests are designed to check an applicant's mental abilities and may involve testing verbal and numerical reasoning.
- Personality tests try to discover an applicant's personality, attitudes and beliefs in an attempt to find out whether he or she will fit well into the business.

Aptitude tests are set if the employer wants to see that the applicant carrying out the sort of tasks involved in doing the job. For example, applicants for a clerical post might be tested on their keyboard skills or telephone technique.

Figure 6.4 Examples of intelligence tests
The diagrams below follow a logical sequence. You are to select the next diagram in the series from the options A–E.

1

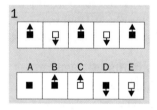

2

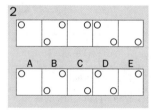

Appointing the person

AQA BS ✓
AQA BCS ✓
EDEXCEL BS ✓
EDEXCEL BC ✓
OCR BS ✓
OCR BCS ✗
WJEC BS ✓
CCEA BS ✓

The contract

When one applicant has been selected and has accepted the position, a **contract of employment** is drawn up. This is an agreement between employer and employee and its terms state the employer's and employee's rights and duties. The contract need not be in writing, but the employee must receive a written statement of the main terms within two months of starting work.

Figure 6.5 A contract of employment

CONTRACT OF EMPLOYMENT

Job title . . . .

employer's name ....   employee's name ....

starting date ....   hours of work ....

pay and pay intervals ....   holidays and holiday pay ....

sickness and sickness pay ....   pension details ....

length of notice required ....   disciplinary rules ....

Ending the appointment

> The government pays redundancy but some businesses have their own agreements giving higher redundancy pay.

Employees may be made **redundant**. This is when their jobs are no longer needed by the business, for example, as a result of changes in work practice or production methods, or changes in demand for goods and services. Staff may receive some redundancy pay; the amount depends on factors such as their length of service, age (for minimum wage) and rate of pay.

An employee can be **dismissed** where there is good reason to do so. Typical situations include stealing the business's goods, where their continued employment would be illegal (e.g. when a lorry driver has been banned from driving), and where their conduct at work deserves dismissal (such as continued drunkenness or violent behaviour). An employee will be given verbal warnings and then written warnings before being dismissed. All employees have protection against **unfair dismissal**.

KEY POINT

Recruitment and selection takes time and is costly, so HR staff must be careful and thorough when employing people.

PROGRESS CHECK

1. List three external sources for obtaining new staff.
2. Name three types of test that might be carried out at interview.

1. JobCentre Plus; recruitment agencies; advertising in newspapers.
2. Intelligence test; personality test; aptitude test.

6.2 Training employees

LEARNING SUMMARY	After studying this section you should be able to understand:
	• the purpose of induction training
	• contents of a typical induction programme
	• the difference between internal and external training
	• advantages and disadvantages of these types of training

Induction training

AQA BS	✓
AQA BCS	✓
EDEXCEL BS	✓
EDEXCEL BC	✓
OCR BS	✓
OCR BCS	✗
WJEC BS	✓
CCEA BS	✓

The HR function has the task of making sure that new employees start working efficiently and productively as soon as possible. To do this, an **induction** training programme is set up. The purpose of induction training is to get the new employees to feel 'at home' as quickly as possible. By doing so, they settle in and soon start making a useful contribution to work. It also provides new employees with a feeling of 'being wanted', which improves levels of morale.

> Induction training introduces the business to the new starter, and the new starter to the business.

A typical induction programme

Here is an example of a typical induction programme:

Figure 6.6 An induction programme

Induction programme for new staff		
DAY	**ACTIVITY**	**VENUE and TIME**
Monday:	Our company's history and present-day activities	Board Room: 10 am
	Tour of the company	Board Room: 11 am
	Lunch	Staff canteen: 1 pm
	The role of Human Resources in your development	Human Resources Dept, Interview room: 2.30 pm
	The work of your Department	Interview room: 3 pm
Tuesday:	Introduction to your Department	Department Manager's office: 9 am
	Meet your new colleagues	Department: 9.30 am

Appraisal

Many organisations use **appraisal schemes** once employees are in the post and gaining experience. These provide the opportunity for managers and employees to assess employee performance, potential and development needs. **Observation** and **interviews** are normally used to appraise employees. Appraisal schemes...

- motivate employees to become more committed to work
- clarify what is expected of an employee and the support the employer can give
- give employees an opportunity to talk about their ideas and hopes
- identify training and career planning needs
- provide information for human resource planning
- assess the suitability of an employee for promotion.

Internal and external training

AQA BS	✓
AQA BCS	✓
EDEXCEL BS	✓
EDEXCEL BC	✓
OCR BS	✓
OCR BCS	✗
WJEC BS	✓
CCEA BS	✓

Once employees become settled in their jobs, further training is offered by Human Resources. This training will either be internal (run within the business) or external.

Internal training

Internal training is also known as 'on-the-job' training where employees learn as they work. The 'teacher' will be the person currently doing the job or an instructor employed by the business. Because internal training takes place at work it is fully **related to the organisation's needs** and also **quick and inexpensive to organise**. It does have the disadvantage that **the training is only as good as the trainers**, who may possess poor training or communication skills and also find that their own work is delayed.

> **KEY POINT**
>
> Internal training can result in good, and bad, working practices being learnt.

External training

'**Off-the-job**' training involves employees attending local colleges or other training providers, and studying to improve their skills. Since training specialists are employed, there should be a **high standard of training**. This type of training **introduces new ideas and techniques** into the business from outside and it is likely to be **more highly regarded by the trainees** if they are studying for a nationally recognised qualification.

External training can be **more expensive** than internal training (although no member of staff has to be released to train the employee) and is not devoted exclusively to the organisation's needs.

Government training

Work Based Learning (WBL) are government-funded schemes which give work-based training to 16–18 year olds and offer apprenticeships and other programmes with a training allowance or wage. Training includes work experience, on-the-job and off-the-job training.

PROGRESS CHECK

1 Why do businesses provide induction training for new employees?
2 State two advantages that internal training has over external training.

2. Related directly to the firm's requirements; inexpensive to organise and carry out.
1. To enable them to settle in quickly and to motivate them.

6.3 Remunerating employees

LEARNING SUMMARY

After studying this section you should be able to understand:
- the different methods of paying employees
- the difference between gross and net pay
- the role of money in motivating staff

Paying employees

AQA BS	✓
AQA BCS	✓
EDEXCEL BS	✓
EDEXCEL BC	✗
OCR BS	✓
OCR BCS	✗
WJEC BS	✓
CCEA BS	✓

Most employees earn either a wage or a salary as a **reward** for their labour. Figure 6.7 shows the typical differences between a 'waged' employee and a 'salaried' employee.

Figure 6.7 Wages and salaries

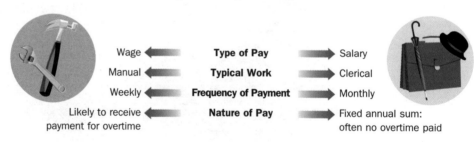

Wage	Type of Pay	Salary
Manual	Typical Work	Clerical
Weekly	Frequency of Payment	Monthly
Likely to receive payment for overtime	Nature of Pay	Fixed annual sum: often no overtime paid

> Profit is the entrepreneur's payment because it is the reward for taking risk.

Reasons for different pay levels

- Doctors, lawyers and many other professional people receive high salaries because of the **level of qualifications** and the **length of training** needed to do this work.
- Pay varies depending on where we are employed in the UK economy, with differences in the pay levels of the private sector (page 19) and the public sector (page 19).
- Pay levels are influenced by the laws of **supply and demand**. People with scarce skills can receive high pay because of the demand for their skills.
- Work varies according to the **danger or discomfort** involved. People employed in dangerous occupations (e.g. oil rig workers) often receive higher pay as a result.

> Many Premier League footballers earn more in a week than most people earn in a year because of high demand for their skills.

- The **location of the work** influences pay levels. For example, some employees living in London and south-east England receive an extra 'London weighting' in their pay because higher living costs mean that employees have to be attracted to, and encouraged to stay in, the high-cost area by being offered higher pay rates.
- The **type of employment** influences the amount and type of pay. Full-time employees receive regular, often fixed, payment whereas temporary, part-time or 'freelance' workers tend to receive varying amounts.
- **Trade unions** influence pay rates: many non-union occupations traditionally receive lower rates of pay.

> The UK's national minimum wage was first paid in 1999, at £3.60 per hour. It had increased to £5.73 per hour by 2009.

KEY POINT

Different levels of pay in an economy are called **wage differentials**.

Payment systems

AQA BS	✓
AQA BCS	✓
EDEXCEL BS	✓
EDEXCEL BC	✗
OCR BS	✓
OCR BCS	✗
WJEC BS	✓
CCEA BS	✓

There are a number of different ways of calculating and paying employees.

Flat-rate

Salaries are normally paid at a **fixed-rate**: one-twelfth of the annual salary is paid into the employee's bank account. Many wages are also paid at a set weekly rate. The advantage to the business is that the individual's pay – and therefore the total wage bill – is easily calculated. The disadvantage to the business is that employees do not have any financial incentive to work harder.

**Figure 6.8
Time rate calculation**

Time-rate

Employees are paid a **set amount per hour** for every hour worked. After a given number of hours have been worked, the employee may be paid at **overtime** rates: 'time and a third', 'time and a half' and 'double time' are commonly paid rates. Figure 6.8 is an example of how an employee's wages are calculated using a time-rate system.

The advantage to a business of this system is that extra work (overtime) is encouraged through extra pay. The disadvantage is that the total wages bill is more difficult to estimate and calculate because there will be more than one hourly rate. This means that the business's administration work is increased because a time recording (e.g. 'clocking in and clocking off') system is needed.

Piece-rate

Employees making items are paid an **agreed amount for each item made**. The items must be of an acceptable quality for pay to be received. Part of their wages may be at a flat rate, with the rest on a piece-rate basis. A popular variation is where sales staff receive commission for each sale they make: the **commission** may also be supported by a 'basic' (flat-rate) pay.

Employees are encouraged to work hard because higher output means higher pay, and efficient and hard-working employees receive more pay than inefficient ones. However, the quality of the output may suffer due to employees rushing their work and so more quality control supervision becomes necessary.

Bonuses and profit-sharing schemes

Employees may receive bonuses during the year, e.g. just before Christmas. Some businesses operate a **merit bonus** scheme, where staff who exceed production or selling targets – or for office staff, those employees who are regarded as being the most efficient – receive a bonus or a higher-than-average pay increase. **Commission** may also be paid, e.g. to sales staff for every product they sell.

Many businesses now have an agreement with the workforce to **give some of the profits** to the employees as a type of bonus. A company's **shares** might also be distributed. These schemes motivate staff by making them feel a part of the business because they are sharing directly in the profits they have helped to create.

Bonus schemes…
- improve business performance
- focus employees' efforts on key objectives, e.g. quality and customer service
- allow employees to share in the success of the business
- increase employee motivation by establishing a link between pay and performance
- are a way of rewarding employees when the business is doing well, without permanently increasing the wage bill.

Bonuses therefore encourage loyalty amongst staff, as well as improving production and sales by setting targets linked to a financial reward. However, a bonus system can lead to disputes – the level of bonus to be awarded can be difficult to calculate, and those employees not receiving the bonus can become dissatisfied.

Figure 6.9 Businesses using employee-share schemes

'All employees can benefit from the wealth they help to create through three share schemes. In the UK we have around 175,000 employees who are also shareholders.' *(Tesco plc Annual Report 2008)*

'Hotel Operations Manager. Up to £22k + profit share' *(Job advert)*

'Substantial increase in basic pay – 25% over the last four years – and "Share in Success" payments of around £1500 have played an important role in motivating the workforce.' *(Royal Mail Group 2007)*

'Today Partners reap the benefit of their year's work, with every Partner receiving a Partnership Bonus worth 20% of salary, the equivalent of 10 weeks' pay. That amounts to a total distribution of £181.1m.' *(John Lewis Partnership, 2008)*

KEY POINT

The method of payment depends mainly on the type of work done; although, more and more businesses now recognise the value of 'employee-share' schemes.

Gross pay and net pay

AQA BS	✓
AQA BCS	✓
EDEXCEL BS	✓
EDEXCEL BC	✗
OCR BS	✓
OCR BCS	✗
WJEC BS	✓
CCEA BS	✓

Figure 6.10 shows how a person's pay is calculated on a time rate basis. The total wage of £328 is the employee's **gross pay**, but the amount of 'take-home' pay is less. There are a series of **deductions** – some voluntary, some compulsory – before the employee receives **net pay**.

Figure 6.10 A payslip

CODE NO.	PAY NO.	NAME		N.I. NO.	Month	
647L	0113611	V. HODGSON		YL324892A	DEC.	**PAY ADVICE**

CUMULATIVE INFORMATION		PAY		DEDUCTIONS	
PAY TO DATE	**SUP'N to DATE**	BASIC	925.00	INCOME TAX	174.50
8471.25	540.75	OVERTIME	14.00	NAT. INS.	61.50
TAX TO DATE	**N. I. TO DATE**	OTHER		SUPERAN.	58.00
1566.50	576.60			OTHER	2.00
GROSS PAY	939.00				
TOTAL DEDUCTIONS	296.00				
NET PAY	643.00	**TOTAL**	939.00	**TOTAL**	296.00

Information on the payslip

- **Code number**: The 'PAYE' (**pay as you earn**) method is normally used to collect income tax. All employees can earn so much free of tax, and their **tax code** (shown by the code number) helps to calculate the correct tax deduction.
- **Deductions**: As well as tax, employees pay **national insurance** towards the cost of the State retirement pension and the National Health Service. Another common deduction is a payment made into a pension scheme (shown as **superannuation** on the payslip). Examples of other deductions are for **trade union subscriptions** and 'SAYE' (**save as you earn**) schemes.

PROGRESS CHECK

1. State two differences between a wage and a salary.
2. List four payment systems.
3. Give two advantages to a business from operating a bonus scheme.

1. Any two from: Wages are paid weekly and salaries monthly; wages associated with manual work, salaries with 'office'; those paid wages are likely to receive overtime payments, salaries are a fixed annual sum.
2. Time-rate; flat-rate; piece-rate; bonuses.
3. Motivates employees by establishing a link between pay and performance; rewards employees when the business is doing well, without permanently increasing the wage bill.

6.4 Motivating employees

After studying this section you should be able to understand:

- why people seek work
- popular theories about motivation
- how a business can create job satisfaction

Human needs and work

AQA BS	✓
AQA BCS	✗
EDEXCEL BS	✓
EDEXCEL BC	✓
OCR BS	✓
OCR BCS	✗
WJEC BS	✓
CCEA BS	✓

There are many different occupations in the UK and we have seen how these occupations can be classified (page 32) into the different sectors of the economy. Regardless of the type of job, the new employee will hope for some **job satisfaction**.

People seek employment for a number of reasons. **Pay** is an important motivator for many employees, but people also want to work for other reasons as well. **Motivation** is important in business because it identifies how satisfied or dissatisfied people are in their work. Employees who are highly motivated tend to work efficiently: if their level of motivation is low, output will suffer and labour disputes may also occur.

Maslow and motivation

There have been many theories put forward in an attempt to explain why people want to work. An American psychologist, **Abraham Maslow**, identified a range of **human needs** that he believed people tried to satisfy. As one type of need became satisfied, another type of need would then require satisfying. He placed these needs in a 'hierarchy', i.e. an order of importance. Figure 6.11 below shows Maslow's five groups of needs.

Figure 6.11 Maslow's hierarchy

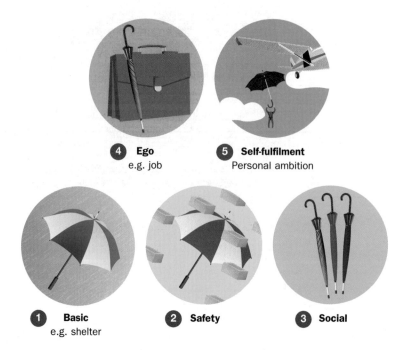

4 Ego
e.g. job

5 Self-fulfilment
Personal ambition

1 Basic
e.g. shelter

2 Safety

3 Social

1. The first **basic** needs are to do with survival and include the need for clothing, warmth and shelter. People also want these basic needs met in the work environment.

2. Once basic needs are satisfied, people's **safety** needs must be met. A person needs to be safe from harm both at home and at work. A safe (secure) job is also important.

3. When basic and safety needs are satisfied, an individual's **social** needs become important. People look for the friendship that comes from being part of a group, such as a group of workmates.

4. Once these three groups of needs are being satisfied, the need to achieve something personal then arises. People have **ego** needs to fulfil. These needs come from a desire for self-esteem, linked to having a job and to making a positive contribution to society.

5. The highest needs are the **self-fulfilment** ones. They involve some form of personal ambition. In the work situation, this could refer to finding great job satisfaction through work that includes a lot of responsibility, or which is highly creative and where its quality and importance is widely recognised.

> The first three needs are sometimes called the 'lower' needs, and the top two are referred to as the 'higher' needs.

According to Maslow – and to most other theorists – **employers need to recognise that there is a range of needs that work must meet**. This means they should provide their employees with jobs that are satisfying in order for output to be at its most efficient.

> **KEY POINT**
>
> Maslow's theory shows the importance of work to individuals and helps explain why unemployment is a major problem where being employed is regarded as 'the norm'.

Herzberg and motivation

Another psychologist, **Frederick Herzberg**, identified what he called **hygiene factors** in work. These are the basic, essential factors such as acceptable working conditions (e.g, safety, cleanliness, adequate rest breaks, control of noise) that form the foundation for having happy and well-motivated employees. Ignoring these hygiene factors will cause morale and motivation to fall, leading to lower output from an unhappy workforce.

Although hygiene factors need to be present at work, Herzberg argued that they do not, by themselves, motivate the employees. The **motivators** for employees include...

- **recognition** – having your efforts at work recognised by people
- **achievement** – the feeling of a 'job well done'
- **advancement** – such as actual (or possible) promotion
- **responsibility** – being given the responsibility to carry out jobs at work.

> **KEY POINT**
>
> To Herzberg, these 'motivators' are the factors that employers should take into account when considering how best to motivate their staff.

Job satisfaction

AQA BS	✓
AQA BCS	✗
EDEXCEL BS	✓
EDEXCEL BC	✓
OCR BS	✓
OCR BCS	✗
WJEC BS	✓
CCEA BS	✓

'Caring' professions such as nursing are examples of careers where employees may not be highly motivated by pay.

Bank and building society employees often receive mortgages and loans at favourable rates.

Different people have different ideas as to what makes a job 'satisfying'. The ideas of Maslow and Herzberg give us some clues about the factors that lead to people enjoying their work. Here are the major influences on job satisfaction:

1. The **pay level** for a job is important. High levels of pay allow employees to buy more material possessions; a high wage can also often compensate for unpleasant working conditions. Many employees will still accept a pay level lower than they could earn elsewhere, since pay is only one of a number of factors.

2. **Fringe benefits**, also known as 'perks', can influence the level of job satisfaction. Popular perks include company cars or subsidised travel, subsidised holidays, private health insurance, and non-contributory (free) pension schemes. Employees may be allowed to buy the company's goods at a discount, or to benefit from its services at discount rates.

3. **Flexible working** may be attractive. Examples include part-time work, flexi-time (where employees have to work within essential 'core time' periods), job sharing, working from home, and shift work.

4. The working **environment** also influences job satisfaction. This includes the level of noise, vibration or dust, the availability and quality of facilities such as canteens, and the degree and effectiveness of heating and ventilation (e.g. whether there is air conditioning).

Other factors influencing job satisfaction include the degree of **job security** and the presence of **friendly colleagues**.

KEY POINT

These factors don't exist in isolation, but combine to give an overall level of satisfaction for a particular job.

PROGRESS CHECK

1. Name the five levels in Maslow's hierarchy of human needs.
2. State three influences on job satisfaction.

1. Basic; Safety; Social; Ego; Self-fulfilment.
2. Pay rate; fringe benefits; working conditions.

6.5 Protecting employees

Employees at work

AQA BS	✓
AQA BCS	✓
EDEXCEL BS	✓
EDEXCEL BC	✗
OCR BS	✓
OCR BCS	✓
WJEC BS	✓
CCEA BS	✓

We already know that an organisation's permanent staff are employed under a contract of employment, which must contain certain information, and employees have the right to receive a written statement of the main terms and conditions of employment.

Working time and time off work

> In the UK we have a longer working week than many EU countries.

The time that employees spend at work is controlled by the **Working Time Regulations**. Most should not have to work more than 48 hours a week on average, and the Regulations include paid holidays, rest and meal breaks.

Employees can request time off work for a number of reasons and might be paid for this time off. Employees also have a statutory (legal) right for certain time off:

- **Leave** – full-time employees are entitled to be paid annual leave of at least 28 days, with the equivalent for part-time employees.

- **Personal reasons** – employees can take reasonable unpaid time off to deal with an emergency involving a dependant, and may need time off for other commitments such as family disputes. Employees will need time off for sickness.
- **Job-related** – employees aged 16–18 are entitled to training or continuing education if they have not reached a given education standard. Someone being made redundant may take time off work to look for another job or arrange training.
- **Work duties** – employees have the right to work-related time off for activities such as health and safety training or trade union duties.
- **Parental reasons** – expectant mothers may be entitled to time off with maternity pay, and fathers or same-sex partners to two weeks' paid leave around the time of birth. Parents are also entitled to at least 13 weeks' unpaid leave per child.
- **Public service** – employees holding certain public positions, such as a member of a local authority or of an educational governing body, are entitled to reasonable unpaid time off; time off for jury service is also allowed.

Equal opportunities at work

Employees must not be victimised, harassed or discriminated against on many grounds: marital status; disability; age; race; sex, sexual orientation or gender reassignment; religion or belief; trade union membership or non-membership; status as a fixed-term or part-time worker. Laws against discriminating include:

- **The Employment Equality (Age) Regulations** make it unlawful to discriminate against workers, employees, jobseekers and trainees because of their age.
- **Under the 1975 Sex Discrimination Act** it is unlawful for an employer to discriminate against someone because of their sex or because they are married.
- **The 1970 Equal Pay Act** makes it unlawful for employers to discriminate between men and women in terms of pay and conditions where they are doing the same or similar work.
- **The Disability Discrimination Act 2005** gives disabled people rights in the areas of employment as well as other areas, such as education and access to facilities.
- **The 1976 Race Relations Act** protects all racial groups, regardless of their race, colour, nationality, religious beliefs, national or ethnic origins, by making it unlawful for an employer to discriminate against someone on racial grounds (race includes colour, nationality, ethnic or national origins).
- It is also against the law for an employer to discriminate on the grounds of religion or certain beliefs.

Laws against discrimination affect all employment areas, including...

- recruitment – the job description, person specification, job advert and application form must not discriminate; interviewers must not ask certain personal questions
- terms, conditions and benefits – men and women are entitled to equal pay for work of equal value
- promotion, transfers, training and dismissal.

Acas (see page 122) or **employment tribunals** hear cases involving employment disputes such as those to do with discrimination. At tribunals, cases are normally heard before a panel of three people, including a legally qualified chairperson.

> Employers are more and more aware of how important it is to operate non-discrimination policies.

KEY POINT

Where an employment tribunal finds that discrimination has occurred penalties are made against the employer.

Health and safety

In 1974 the **Health and Safety at Work Act** (HASAWA) was passed. HASAWA states the duties of the employer and the employee regarding health and safety at work. Employees are entitled to a safe system of work and a safe working environment.

The employer's duties	The employee's duties
to provide safe: • **working conditions** • **machinery** • **working processes** • **entry and exit arrangements**	• to take **reasonable care of themselves and others** whilst at work • **not to interfere** with anything provided for their own safety or the safety of others • to **report any defects** in equipment, work areas etc. • to **co-operate with the employer** over health and safety matters

The employer might have specific health and safety duties for particular types of equipment. One example is safe computer use, where the employer must make sure workstations meet safety requirements and plan work so there are breaks or changes in the type of work done.

As well as duties under HASAWA, an employee also has rights. These are to have rest breaks, to see that risks to their health and safety are properly controlled, and to stop work if there are reasonable doubts about safety.

Work organisations

AQA BS	✓
AQA BCS	✓
EDEXCEL BS	✓
EDEXCEL BC	✗
OCR BS	✓
OCR BCS	✓
WJEC BS	✓
CCEA BS	✓

Trade unions

Because individual employees are not in a powerful position, they often act together as a single unit – a **union** – to protect their interests at work, to protect their **jobs**, or to improve their **pay** and **working conditions**.

All unions carry out activities to benefit their members. Their main aims are as follows:

1. To **negotiate with employers**. This bargaining will be mainly to do with pay and bonuses, hours, working conditions, and pensions. Unions are interested in **job satisfaction**, and **job security** will be negotiated. **Collective bargaining** is the normal way in which pay and conditions are agreed, with union officials representing groups of workers.
2. To **protect their members** against unfair dismissal, possible lay-offs and redundancy. Part-time workers may also be represented and protected by the union. A union may also have to figure out how to give members the rights to which they are entitled, for equal pay and treatment for women, and against other forms of discrimination.
3. To **advise and represent** their members. Unions often provide personal support and legal advice on problems at work.
4. To **influence others**. Unions seek to influence employers, employer organisations and the government in order to benefit their members.

Workers joining a trade union will pay a subscription. For this, they receive a number of benefits from their union membership.

Figure 6.12 Benefits of trade union membership

Disputes

Collective bargaining does not always succeed and disputes involving **industrial action** can still occur. A union may take different forms of industrial action:

- With **overtime bans**, the union instructs its members not to work overtime: this leads to falling output and puts pressure on the employer to agree to the union's demands.
- In a **work-to-rule**, employees follow the 'rule book' very closely, which can slow down or even halt production; a **go-slow** is similar, occurring when members carry out their work more slowly than normal.
- Employees may have **sit-ins**, occupying the buildings to stop goods entering or leaving. Most sit-ins take place when there is a threat to close the business.

The last resort is for union members to go on **strike** and withdraw their labour. This isn't a popular strategy with unions because members lose pay, there may be legal problems, and it can result in the business closing with employees permanently losing work.

The dispute may be settled by the action of one or both of the parties to it. The government may also put some pressure on the parties to end the dispute. If the dispute carries on for some time, **Acas** (Advisory, Conciliation and Arbitration Service) may become involved. Acas was set up to improve industrial relations. It is independent from both employers and unions and offers various services:

1 **Conciliation** and **mediation**. An Acas official talks to both sides to find areas of 'common ground', which then form the basis for further negotiations.
2 **Arbitration**. If both sides agree, their dispute 'goes to arbitration'. Acas provides an independent third party to listen to the points made, and offers a settlement.

> Other Acas services include publishing guidelines and 'codes of practice' on industrial relations.

Figure 6.13 Acas's vision statement

> Acas's vision is to be Britain's champion for successful workplaces and a motivated workforce.

PROGRESS CHECK

1 Identify four aims of trade unions.
2 List four forms of industrial action that union members may take.

1. Negotiate with employers; protect members; advise and represent members; influence others.
2. Go-slows; overtime bans; working-to-rule; strikes.

Sample GCSE questions

Tasty Juice Ltd makes fruit drinks that are sold in supermarkets. *Tasty Juice Ltd* needs to recruit a Personal Assistant for the Chairman. The HR staff must create a job description and a person specification for this position, and place a job advertisement in the local paper.

(a) Give one reason why the HR staff should create a job description.

A job description is created so that people can see what the job involves. **(2)**

(b) Describe **two** items of information that should appear in this job description.

Hours of work: when the PA has to be there (start and finish times). Pay (how much each week). **(4)**

(c) Explain why it is important to prepare a person specification for this position.

So that Tasty Juice Ltd can see if the applicants are OK for the post. **(4)**

(d) Why should *Tasty Juice Ltd* interview shortlisted candidates for this position?

So they could talk to the candidates to see if they are any good at the job of Personal Assistant. **(2)**

(e) Outline two other ways *Tasty Juice Ltd* could use to select a person for this position.

Tasty Juice Ltd could use an employment agency to get them a suitable person. Tasty Juice Ltd could use tests to make sure the person can do the job. **(4)**

(f) Explain how government legislation affects *Tasty Juice Ltd's* recruitment procedures.

Government legislation is when laws are passed to do with employing people, protecting against race, sex, age and disability discrimination so that Tasty Juice Ltd will be fair and legal when it comes to employing people. **(4)**

This is rather vague: you need to give specific examples such as, 'It outlines the duties and responsibilities of the position' and 'It helps the applicant to study exactly what is involved'.

These are good examples (though an annual salary, rather than a weekly wage, is more likely to be given for this position).

'OK' is not business-like: be precise, pointing out, that the person spec helps to shortlist, and is used in the interview to discuss the applicant's suitability.

Interviews check the candidate's suitability, to select the best person, to check information provided on the application form, and to allow a two-way conversation.

Incorrect: employment agencies recruit (not select) people. You should explain two of the various tests (personality, aptitude and intelligence) that the company can use in selection.

The basis of a good answer because it mentions important areas (race, age, sex and disability). However, the candidate should explain the effect of these laws, for example, do not advertise for a 'female only' PA.

Exam practice questions

1 *Garfield Print* uses computers to design items such as wedding stationery, posters and catalogues for its customers. It is going to recruit a new employee to design posters and catalogues using the latest computer technology. Each applicant has been asked to send a Curriculum Vitae (CV) and a letter of application prepared on a computer.

(a) **(i)** What is a Curriculum Vitae?

.... **(2)**

(ii) In selecting candidates for this particular job, explain why *Garfield Print* is likely to want computer-printed material to help it select the new employee.

....

.... **(2)**

(b) *Garfield Print* has received ten applications and has decided to use testing as another way of selecting the person for the job.

(i) Describe two methods by which *Garfield Print* could test the applicants for the job.

....

.... **(4)**

(ii) Select one of these methods and explain how it will help *Garfield Print* to recruit the best applicant.

....

.... **(2)**

(c) *Garfield Print* will interview five applicants. Why is an interview a suitable way to make the final selection of the new employee?

....

.... **(4)**

(d) **(i)** What is the purpose of a contract of employment?

.... **(2)**

(ii) State four items that will be contained in the contract of employment for the successful applicant.

....

.... **(4)**

7 Operations management

The following topics are covered in this chapter:

- Methods of production
- Economies of scale
- Productivity
- Stock and quality

7.1 Methods of production

LEARNING SUMMARY

After studying this section you should be able to understand:

- the main methods of production
- what 'lean' production is
- how production becomes lean

How production is organised

AQA BS	✓
AQA BCS	✗
EDEXCEL BS	✓
EDEXCEL BC	✗
OCR BS	✓
OCR BCS	✗
WJEC BS	✓
CCEA BS	✓

Job production

Job production occurs when a business makes a **single unique product** from start to finish. The 'job' is based on the customer's **individual requirements**, so...

- skilled labour is often used, with high labour costs due to the work being **labour-intensive**
- employees have to be versatile, able to use a variety of tools and equipment
- economies of scale (pages 128–129) are not possible as the finished product is often expensive.

> Ships and bridges are examples of job production.

Businesses using job production often find it difficult to accurately calculate the 'three Cs': the total **cost** of the job, the **cashflows** from it, and the job's **completion date**.

Figure 7.1 Job production: O2 Arena in London

Examples of batch production include building similar houses on an estate and making different styles of clothing.

Examples of flow production include cars and consumer durable goods.

Batch production

Similar products are made in 'blocks' or batches. Production staff must make two key decisions: **how many** to make in each batch (to control costs) and **in what order** the different batches should be made.

Flow production

The products made using the flow production method pass straight from one stage of production to the next. Types of flow production include **mass** and **process** production. **Large numbers of identical, standardised products** are made as cheaply as possible, and economies of scale keep costs down. A business using flow production will...

- be **capital-intensive**, using specialist machinery and equipment
- employ people who specialise in using specialist equipment
- use **automated** production lines that work **continuously** (e.g. by shift work)
- be making high-demand products for a mass market
- rely on its marketing function to help sell the mass production.

Figure 7.2 Mass production of milk cartons

> **KEY POINT**
>
> The method of production used depends on the **scale** of production involved.

Lean production

AQA BS	✓
AQA BCS	✗
EDEXCEL BS	✓
EDEXCEL BC	✗
OCR BS	✓
OCR BCS	✗
WJEC BS	✓
CCEA BS	✓

*Flow production causes problems for businesses. Employees become bored and suffer from low morale. Labour and machinery is over-specialised so the business finds it difficult to respond to changes in its market. Equipment failure or employee action such as strikes are costly because production can be brought to a halt.

These drawbacks of flow production have led to **lean production** being used by many businesses. Lean production sets out to...

- **reduce costs**, such the as costs of holding stock, and **improve quality** (page 134)
- **improve staff morale** and therefore employee **productivity levels**
- **use capacity efficiently** (page 130).

A firm's approach to lean production may be based on **cell production**, the **Kaizen** philosophy, and 'Just-In-Time' (**JIT**).

*Employees are also less skilled than those on job production, which can cause problems if they lose their jobs.

Cell production

Staff in each cell feel they are much more involved in the overall production.

The cell production approach has developed from mass manufacture. It tries to overcome the problems of low morale that can affect employees working on mass production lines. Cell production divides the production line into different 'cells'. Each cell is a self-contained unit that produces an identifiable part of the finished product.

Kaizen

Kaizen is a Japanese term and its ideas have become popular with many UK businesses. It is based on the belief that it is often **better to invest in the views and ideas of staff rather than in new resources**, such as new equipment. The Kaizen approach also accepts that employees will also **look for ways to improve their work**.

The Kaizen approach is not limited to production and can extend throughout the business.

Groups are set up to put the Kaizen approach into practice, discussing production and other issues and offering solutions. For example, a shop-floor production cell may operate as a Kaizen team.

Just-In-Time (JIT)

The Just-In-Time approach, also influenced by Japanese work practices, **tries to reduce stockholding costs**. This is achieved when the business operates with no buffer (reserve) stocks.

The **kanban** order card system is an example of JIT. Assume that a firm makes its own packaging. When made, this packaging is moved to the packing section where it is kept in two containers. When one container is empty it, with its kanban card, is taken to where the packaging is made. Packaging starts being made to go in this container, 'just-in-time', for when it is needed by the finished products (as the second container becomes empty).

Advantages of JIT	Disadvantages of JIT
Holding and storage costs fall	Costs of ordering increase
There will be less stock wastage	The business relies on its suppliers
Cash-flow (liquidity) improves	A delivery problem will stop production

KEY POINT

Lean production can lead to more products made more cheaply with fewer resources: this makes the business more competitive.

PROGRESS CHECK

1. Which of the following products would normally be produced using flow production techniques?
(a) Bridges (b) Made-to-measure double-glazing (c) Paving slabs (d) TVs (e) Cars.
2. What does efficient 'Just-In-Time' production depend on?

1. (d) TVs and (e) cars. (a) Bridges and (b) double glazing illustrate job production. (c) paving slabs are likely to be made in batches.
2. For JIT to work efficiently, a business needs close working relationships with its suppliers because frequent deliveries of quality stocks are needed.

7.2 Economies of scale

LEARNING SUMMARY

After studying this section you should be able to understand:
- internal and external economies of scale
- diseconomies of scale

Internal and external economies of scale

AQA BS	✓
AQA BCS	✗
EDEXCEL BS	✓
EDEXCEL BC	✗
OCR BS	✓
OCR BCS	✗
WJEC BS	✓
CCEA BS	✓

Internal economies of scale

Internal economies of scale arise from something that happens inside the business that reduces its average costs. How do average costs fall? As output increases and the scale of operation grows, this increased output does not normally increase the fixed costs (page 88). These fixed costs are spread over the larger output, so average cost per unit falls. For example, if a business pays £100 000 rent each year and...

- last year 50 000 items were made, average fixed cost is £2 per item
- this year 100 000 items are made, the average fixed cost falls to £1 per item.

The main internal economies of scale leading to lower unit costs are...

- **economies of increased dimensions** – these arise from increased size; for example, oil company 'supertankers' have up to 20 times the capacity of smaller ships, yet cost only three or four times as much to build and run
- **financial economies** – larger businesses are assumed to be more stable financially and it is easier to borrow finance and to negotiate lower interest rates
- **managerial economies** – well-qualified experts can be employed by larger businesses, and the cost of management does not increase at the same rate as output; a larger business still only has one managing director
- **marketing economies** – larger businesses can afford to use specialist firms such as advertising agencies; advertising is spread over more sales, reducing unit cost
- **purchasing economies** – larger businesses receive bulk-buying discounts and can negotiate more favourable (cheaper) credit terms with suppliers
- **risk-bearing economies** – increasing the product range brings diversification, which spreads the risk across more markets and more products
- **technical economies** – large-scale production means more efficient and advanced machinery can be used; a larger firm can also afford to invest in **research and development** to improve its products.

> Bulk buying illustrates how economies of scale occur when variable costs (per unit) fall – the price per unit is lower.

Figure 7.3 Economy of increased dimensions

KEY POINT

Internal economies of scale result from a **falling average cost per unit.**

External economies of scale

When the whole **industry** grows in size, its businesses benefit from external economies of scale:

- **Concentration** – an industry based mainly in one area encourages suppliers to locate to the same area.
- **Skilled staff** – local labour and management gain specialist skills.
- **Reputation** – a good local or regional reputation helps businesses in that area and encourages other businesses to locate there.
- **Information** – businesses in the area may jointly provide information schemes, supported by their local trade associations and chambers of commerce.

> Examples include 'Sheffield steel', 'Potteries' china, and financial services (London).

Diseconomies of scale

Although there are many benefits that come from increased size, there are limits to these benefits. A business may grow too large and start to suffer from **diseconomies** as its **unit costs increase**. These diseconomies arise for a number of reasons, for example, as a result of over-long communication channels or through increased bureaucracy (red tape').

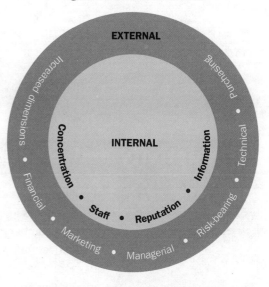

Figure 7.4. Economies of scale

Figure 7.5. Diseconomies of scale

The larger the firm, the more levels of hierarchy ('tall structures') there can be

Bringing about

greater bureaucracy ('red tape') due to a longer chain of command

Which may result in

a lack of personal contact between management and the rest of the workforce

Causing

employee dissatisfaction and poor labour relations

Which may lead to

low morale, higher absenteeism and lower efficiency

KEY POINT

The larger the business the more levels of hierarchy there tend to be for communication to flow through; this leads to greater bureaucracy.

PROGRESS CHECK

1. Distinguish between internal and external economies of scale.
2. How can economies of scale occur if total costs increase when a business expands?

1. Internal economies of scale are within the business. External economies of scale occur when all firms in the area benefit, such as having a local supply of skilled labour.
2. Although total costs increase, the average cost per unit falls because the fixed costs are spread over a larger output and/or because it is gaining from cheaper unit variable costs (such as by bulk-buying).

7.3 Productivity

LEARNING SUMMARY

After studying this section you should be able to understand:

- the importance of productivity to a business
- how technology can be used efficiently

Productivity and productive capacity

AQA BS	✓
AQA BCS	✗
EDEXCEL BS	✓
EDEXCEL BC	✗
OCR BS	✓
OCR BCS	✗
WJEC BS	✓
CCEA BS	✓

A business's **productivity** tells us **how efficient it is at producing its products**. We can measure the productivity of the workforce, for example, by measuring the average number of products made per employee. Businesses also measure how productive their other resources are. A business's **productive capacity** refers to its resources, in particular, its premises, the machinery and equipment it has, and its workforce. If all are working at their maximum output, the business is said to be operating at **full capacity**.

Working at or near full capacity can, however, create problems for a business. There is increased pressure…

- on **staff**, which can lead to greater absenteeism, e.g. as a result of stress caused by high workloads
- on **equipment**; extra use causes greater wear and tear, leading to equipment breakdown that affects production
- if **even more work** is taken on – if the business is working at or near full capacity it is difficult to find additional capacity.

> Businesses in this situation often employ more part-time staff (e.g. seasonal workers) or hire / buy extra premises and equipment.

Other businesses may have to **reduce excess capacity**. This becomes necessary when demand for their products falls, either temporarily due to the economy being in recession, or permanently, e.g. when consumer tastes have changed. Ways of reducing excess staff include making employees **redundant** (forced to leave their job voluntarily or compulsorily) and through 'natural wastage' (not replacing leavers). Non-human resources will be reduced, for example, by moving to smaller and cheaper premises.

> **KEY POINT**
>
> Production tries to turn **input into output** as efficiently as possible: this is a measure of the business's productivity.

Using technology efficiently

> The nature of work - e.g. skills, training - changes as a business's use of technology changes.

It is important for technology to be as productive as possible. Many businesses use advanced technologies in the production process, for example…

- **computer-aided design** (CAD) – computers create efficient product designs that can be altered immediately, e.g. by using light pens or touch-sensitive screens
- **computer-aided manufacture** (CAM) – robotics and other forms of automation are used to make products efficiently
- **computer-integrated manufacturing** (CIM) – computers control the entire production process, linking with other areas of work such as design and planning, purchasing, stock control and distribution.

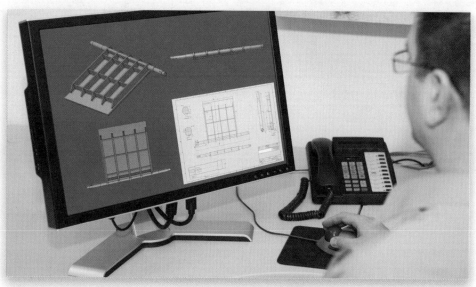

Designer using a CAD machine

PROGRESS CHECK

1. What is the difference between production and productivity?
2. What are the resources involved when measuring productive capacity?

1. 'Production' refers to how many (and what types) are made; 'productivity' refers to how efficient the business is at making what it does make.
2. Productive capacity measures the use of human resources and non-human resources such as buildings and equipment.

7.4 Stock and quality

Buying stock

AQA BS	✓
AQA BCS	✗
EDEXCEL BS	✓
EDEXCEL BC	✗
OCR BS	✓
OCR BCS	✗
WJEC BS	✓
CCEA BS	✓

Manufacturing and non-manufacturing businesses make many types of purchases. The purchases made by a typical purchasing department are shown in Figure 7.6.

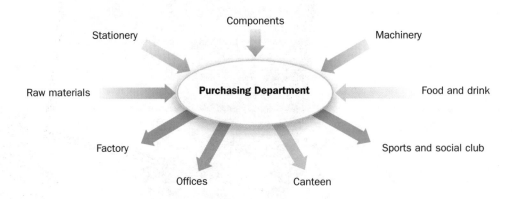

Figure 7.6 Role of the purchasing department

The main role of the purchasing department is therefore **materials management**. The items must be bought ...

- at the **correct price**
- at the **correct level of quality**
- in the **correct quantities** and delivered at the **correct time** to the **correct place**.

Stock control

AQA BS	✓
AQA BCS	✗
EDEXCEL BS	✓
EDEXCEL BC	✗
OCR BS	✓
OCR BCS	✗
WJEC BS	✓
CCEA BS	✓

A business has to hold sufficient stocks for a number of reasons.

Stock item	Reason	Costs of zero stock
• Raw materials and work in progress	• To meet production requirements	• Idle time (worker and machine); knock-on effect of delayed production
• Finished goods	• To meet customer demand	• Loss of goodwill and orders; financial penalties for missing deadlines
• Consumables, spares, equipment	• To support sales and production	• Idle time (worker and machine); delayed production

> Stock rotation is particularly important with perishable stock such as food.

Businesses must also manage their stock efficiently. The oldest stock will normally be used first (stock rotation) and stock wastage must be minimised.

In any business there are conflicting 'pulls' that influence buying and stock control policies. Purchasing departments must balance the need to keep costs under control with ensuring that stock is always available.

Figure 7.7 The 'pulls' in stock control

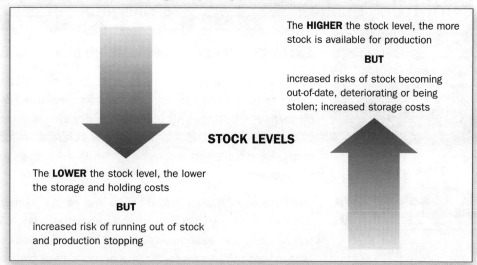

The **HIGHER** the stock level, the more stock is available for production

BUT

increased risks of stock becoming out-of-date, deteriorating or being stolen; increased storage costs

STOCK LEVELS

The **LOWER** the stock level, the lower the storage and holding costs

BUT

increased risk of running out of stock and production stopping

Optimum stock

The optimum stock (the best stock level) is the level that **minimises costs**. There are four control levels used to calculate optimum stock:

1. **Reorder level** – the stock level at which a new order will be made.
2. **Minimum stock** – the **buffer** stock level, below which the stock level should not fall.
3. **Maximum stock** – this is the highest level of stock that will be held.
4. **Reorder quantity** – the **Economic Order Quantity** (EOQ) is the number of items of stock that will be reordered once the reorder stock level has been reached. The EOQ is calculated by comparing the costs the business would face by holding a lot of stock, with the savings it gets from buying this stock in bulk.

The EOQ calculation is based on a number of 'constants': a **constant demand** for the stock, a **constant lead time** (time between placing an order and receiving it), and **constant costs of making an order**.

Stock control charts can be constructed to show these levels.

Figure 7.8 A stock control chart

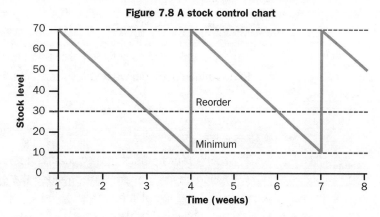

The **Just-In-Time** (JIT) approach (page 127) aims to reduce stockholding costs by cutting stock to a minimum. Stock items are delivered when they are needed and are used immediately.

(page 127)

KEY POINT

A business using the JIT approach faces the risk of running out of stock, so it must be confident that its suppliers are able to deliver on demand.

Quality

Quality control forms an important part of production control.

Quality assurance and quality control

Customer satisfaction is necessary for business success. **Quality assurance** seeks to achieve this by agreeing and **implementing quality standards** throughout a business. The use of **quality circles** – closely linked to the Kaizen philosophy (page 127) – is an example of quality assurance. Quality circles are employee groups with a common interest, who meet to discuss quality-related work issues.

The purpose of **quality control** is to ensure that **standards are being maintained**. It is particularly associated with traditional flow-line production. A recent trend has been for employees to adopt a **self-checking** approach: this is an example of the **people-centred management** philosophy that quality is the responsibility of all employees.

Quality control sets out to…
- **prevent** problems from happening in the first place
- **detect** and **correct** quality problems before the goods reach the customer
- **improve** quality to meet higher customer expectations.

Quality initiatives

Benchmarking measures a business's production or other activity against the **industry standard**. It looks for 'best practice' from other businesses and managers compare this practice to that in their business. By using benchmarking…
- managers can set **realistic targets**
- employees become **motivated** through greater involvement.

Total Quality Management (TQM) seeks to establish a **quality culture** to guarantee the quality of work by all employees at all stages. It is a philosophy associated with quality circles and which emphasises the importance of after-sales service.

KEY POINT

The more efficient businesses believe that it is better to 'get it right first time' to avoid the costs, delays and loss of orders that come from getting it wrong.

PROGRESS CHECK

1. Name four items that a typical manufacturing business must buy.
2. A purchasing department provides the correct items in the correct _____ , at the correct _____ and the correct _____ , and delivered to the correct _____ .

1. **Any suitable answers, e.g.** Raw materials; office stationery; manufacturing machinery; company cars.   2. Quantity; price / time; time / price; place

Sample GCSE questions

This question is about methods of production, stock and quality control.

The *Ice Cream Farm* makes and sells a range of ice cream and frozen yogurt products. It is still based next to the owner's farm, from where it gets some of its ingredients. The business has sold its products locally for many years. Nowadays it uses specialised production lines. The packing process uses the flow method, but produces identifiable batches of flavoured yogurt and ice cream. Quality control is important and the owner has introduced computers to help control the production process and stock levels in the factory shop and warehouse.

(a) Using examples, explain the terms below:

(i) batch production

Batch production is where a number of the same things are made at a time. Examples include wallpaper, lamp shades and garden furniture. **(3)**

(ii) flow production

Flow production involves making things all the time. It is widely found in the UK. Examples include making chemicals, liquids such as petrol from oil refining, and the sort of things you buy in `do-it-yourself` stores. **(3)**

(b) Why should the *Ice Cream Farm* be so concerned about quality control?

Where a company is making things such as ice cream, or other food and drinks, it has to be very careful to ensure that they are safe to eat and drink. If the Ice Cream Farm finds that it is making ice cream that isn't safe to eat, it will lose a lot of custom and may go out of business. **(4)**

(c) Why does the *Ice Cream Farm* have to control its stocks?

The Ice Cream Farm must monitor its stocks because it needs to make sure that it does not have too much stock, nor too little. The effect of Ice Cream Farm having too much stock is that money is wasted in holding all this stock; space that could be used for other things is tied up with stock, and because of the nature of the stocks they may go off or even be stolen. If the business has too little stock, it may not have enough to keep making more using a continuous flow process. **(6)**

This definition only just explains batch production. It should mention that, once one batch is completed, another batch of a different product is made. Relevant examples but not used well in the answer.

You should give a clearer definition. Mention the mass production aspect and how products made pass straight from one process to the next. Also include features such as being capital-intensive. Good examples to start with, but reference to DIY stores is vague so give examples from these stores such as light bulbs, nails, paints.

A good start, though more could be made of selling poor quality products in general – customers look elsewhere, switch to competitor brands, market share is lost, profits fall and survival of the firm is in question.

Relevant points about overstocking, quite well explained. With too few stocks, explain the effect of not being able to meet production targets: loss of deliveries = loss of sales orders and future orders, with customers turning elsewhere.

Exam practice questions

This is a question on methods of production and economies of scale.

1   *Getbilt* is a manufacturer of modern household furniture. The company is moving to a new factory. The Managing Director of *Getbilt* has to decide on the method of production to be used to make the products in the new factory.

(a)   **(i)** State how the furniture would be made if the Managing Director decided on job production.

....

....   **(2)**

(ii) Explain one advantage and one disadvantage to *Getbilt* if the company uses job production to make the furniture.

....

....

....

....   **(4)**

(b)   Explain why, if flow production is used, *Getbilt* is likely to benefit from economies of scale.

....

....

....

....

....   **(6)**

(c)   Which method should the Managing Director choose? Give reasons for your answer

....

....

....

....   **(4)**

8 Business communication

The following topics are covered in this chapter:

- **The communication model**
- **Types of business communication**
- **Successful business communication**
- **Communicating with stakeholders**

8.1 The communication model

LEARNING SUMMARY

After studying this section you should be able to understand:

- the purpose and process of business communication
- how communication in business can be formal or informal

The nature of communication

AQA BS	✗
AQA BCS	✓
EDEXCEL BS	✓
EDEXCEL BC	✓
OCR BS	✓
OCR BCS	✓
WJEC BS	✓
CCEA BS	✗

The **purpose** of communication is to **transmit information** from one person or group to another. Managers and employees in business need to be aware of the nature of communication and of the special skills required when communicating information.

Communication involves two parties: the **sender** and the **recipient** (the **receiver**). The **process** of communication involves the following stages:

> The method that the sender uses to communicate the information will affect how the information is interpreted by the receiver.

1 The sender **selecting a communication method** to use, for example, choosing to deliver the information by speech or in a written form.

2 The sender **transmitting information** using this method, supported by a communication medium such as a telephone or computer email.

3 The recipient of the communication **receiving the information** being communicated.

4 The recipient **giving feedback** to the sender that the communication has been received.

Formal and informal communication

AQA BS	✗
AQA BCS	✓
EDEXCEL BS	✓
EDEXCEL BC	✓
OCR BS	✓
OCR BCS	✓
WJEC BS	✓
CCEA BS	✗

Communication takes place both **internally** (within the business) and **externally** (between the business and another organisation). Most businesses, especially the larger ones, have **formal communication** channels. These are shown on the business's **organisation chart** (page 54), which is often displayed in the form of a **hierarchy**.

Organisation charts can also be constructed to show different structures and layouts, for example, the matrix structure (page 55). Other examples include...

- the **circular** organisation chart – this presents the business organisation in the form of a circle rather than as a list (as shown by the hierarchical chart), which helps the business organise its resources and communication systems efficiently
- the **flat** organisation chart – this displays an organisational structure with few levels between managers and other employees; such organisations often have efficient communication as a result of these fewer layers.

KEY POINT

Specialist or general software such as Microsoft Visio and PowerPoint are used to draw these charts.

The main trading documents

Businesses involved in buying and selling record their transactions using formal documents. These trading documents act as a **record** of events and as **proof** that a transaction has taken place.

Documents flow between the buyer and the seller, as shown in Figure 8.1 below.

Figure 8.1 Trading Document Flow

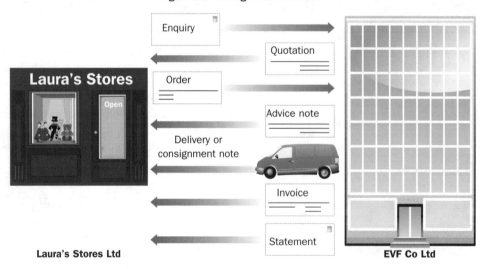

Laura's Stores

Enquiry

Quotation

Order

Advice note

Delivery or consignment note

Invoice

Statement

Laura's Stores Ltd   EVF Co Ltd

On receiving a **letter of enquiry** the selling business sends product details. If the buyer is interested a **quotation** may be asked for; this is sent by the seller, often with a catalogue and price list. The **order** sent by the buyer indicates...

- the number of items ordered
- their description, catalogue number and price
- when and where they are to be delivered.

The supplier may forward an **advice note** separately from the goods to tell the buyer they have been despatched. A **delivery note** is sent when the supplier delivers the goods (a **consignment note** may be sent if an independent carrier delivers them).

The **invoice** contains details of the goods – their description, quantity, price and total cost – and the buyer may treat the invoice as a bill for payment. Several copies are often produced (for the seller's accounts, sales and despatch departments), the top copy going to the buyer.

If the buyer is a regular customer, the seller will send at a later date a **statement of account** showing the goods sent and payments received in the period.

Figure 8.2 An invoice

EVF Co Ltd
Highbridge Road, Wellington, Somerset TA1 2ER
Telephone (01952) 459741 Fax (01952) 459842

To: Laura's Stores Ltd
Taunton Road   Date: 19.8.09
Burnham-on-Sea
Somerset LS7 8EF   Order No.: 160180

PROD. CODE	QUANTITY AND DESCRIPTION	UNIT PRICE £	p	TOTAL £	p
EV8	10 'Foxy' cuddly toys	2	50	25	00
TD2	12 'Tina' dolls	12	00	144	00
				169	00
	Less: Trade discount 10%			16	90
				152	10
	Value Added Tax at 17½%			26	62
			TOTAL DUE	178	72

Terms: 2½% 28 days
E&OE   VAT Reg. 403-8871-988

KEY POINT

The invoice is the most important document used in trading.

Informal communication

Informal communication takes place in all organisations. This communication is normally oral and can also be expressed through body language, such as a gesture or a glance. It often exists when groups of employees work together.

Informal communication can bring benefits to an organisation by giving people the chance to express their feelings and concerns. However, because it is informal, this type of communication can lead to mistrust and misunderstanding through, for example, communicating rumours rather than facts. Informal communication is often called 'the grapevine'.

KEY POINT

The feedback the receiver gives the sender on whether the message has been understood and used will measure the success of the communication process.

PROGRESS CHECK

1 What is the purpose of business communication?
2 Name the two parties involved in business communication.

1. To transmit information. 2. The sender; the receiver.

8.2 Types of business communication

LEARNING SUMMARY

After studying this section you should be able to understand:

- the nature, main types, strength and weaknesses of...
  - oral communication
  - written communication
  - visual communication

Oral communication

AQA BS	✗
AQA BCS	✓
EDEXCEL BS	✓
EDEXCEL BC	✓
OCR BS	✓
OCR BCS	✓
WJEC BS	✓
CCEA BS	✗

Oral communication can be both formal and informal and is most appropriate for transmitting simple, low-volume information quickly. Face-to-face and telephone communication are the most common forms. Oral communication does not provide a written record of what was said and agreed.

Oral communication has several advantages over written communication. It is...
- a **two-way process** – the receiver is part of the conversation
- a **quick method** of transmitting information – it has immediate impact
- **flexible** – points can be queried.

> Perhaps the most important meeting is a company's AGM because directors are elected and the company's performance is discussed.

There are three popular ways of communicating orally in business:
- **Meetings** follow formal procedures with the order of business being shown on the meeting **agenda** (page 142). **Minutes** (page 142) are taken to ensure that there is a written record of events. Examples of formal meetings include a company's **Annual General Meeting** (AGM: page 149) and board meetings. Examples of more informal business meetings include quality circles (page 134) that do not have formal agendas, or minutes taken.
- **Presentations** are sometimes used in formal situations, for example, a press conference or training session. They provide structured information and are often supported by non-verbal information, such as on charts or graphs.

Presentation

Non-verbal communication

- **Interviews** (page 108) are another formal method of oral communication. They are widely used by the Human Resources function, for example, when selecting new staff or when carrying out grievance or disciplinary procedures.

Non-verbal communication (NVC) is important in both formal and informal communication. NVC includes the use of facial expressions, eye contact, tone of voice, gestures, body contact, and physical appearance and closeness. The communicator needs to ensure that any **non-verbal signals** support the oral message.

> **KEY POINT**
>
> In face-to-face communication, if the non-verbal and the spoken communications do not support each other, the flow of communication is hindered.

Written communication

AQA BS	X
AQA BCS	✓
EDEXCEL BS	✓
EDEXCEL BC	✓
OCR BS	✓
OCR BCS	✓
WJEC BS	✓
CCEA BS	X

Written communication tends to be used when **high-volume** or **technical** information needs to be transmitted. Once popularly used in business when speed was not important, the development and popularity of technology now allows written business communication to be transmitted very quickly, for example, by email.

Written communication is often most appropriate when a **formal, long-term record of the information is needed**, and when this information needs to be kept and used in later communication. Popular examples are given below.

Figure 8.3 A memo

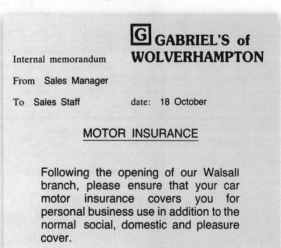

Internal memorandum

G GABRIEL'S of WOLVERHAMPTON

From Sales Manager

To Sales Staff   date: 18 October

MOTOR INSURANCE

Following the opening of our Walsall branch, please ensure that your car motor insurance covers you for personal business use in addition to the normal social, domestic and pleasure cover.

Figure 8.4 Sections in Marks and Spencer Plc's Annual Report 2008

YOUR M&S
Annual Report 2008

- Home
- About us
- Chairman's foreword
- Chief Executive's statement
- Group Finance and Operations
- Director's statement
- Building our brand
- Business review
- Financial review
- Governance
- Remuneration report
- Financial statements
- Shareholder Information

- **Memorandum** – the 'memo' is **informal** and **summary** by nature and is the main **internal** written form used in organisations, for example sent from a departmental head to employees about a new development.
- **Business letter** – the main **external** form of written communication. The letter is **more formal**, although it can be used internally (e.g. to make a formal statement to an employee).
- **Manual** – a manual is a written summary of technical information and procedures, for example, a budget manual.
- **Report** – a report provides detailed written information of activities such as market research, or the financial performance of a company (e.g. its Annual Report). Many company reports are supported by video on the company's website, to help explain the information.
- **Notice** – an organisation's notice board allows written information to be displayed for as long as is required.
- **Newsletter** – the newsletter is a popular method of circulating and updating employees on a regular basis.
- **Agenda and minutes** – used in connection with formal meetings, the agenda summarises the structure and contents of the meeting, and the minutes act as a formal written summary of what was said and agreed at the meeting.

A typical meeting agenda

1. **Introductions and apologies for absence**

2. **Minutes of the previous meeting**
   (People at the meeting examine the minutes of the previous meeting and either agree with them or ask for changes to be made.)

3. **Matters arising**
   (Any subjects in the minutes of the previous meeting where updated information is available will be dealt with here.)

4. **Reports**
   (The main bulk of the agenda is taken up with reports presented, or information discussed, at the meeting.)

5. **Any other business**
   (If there is any other business that arrived too late to be included on the agenda it may, at the Chair's discretion, be discussed here.)

6. **Date of next meeting**

Visual communication

AQA BS	✗
AQA BCS	✓
EDEXCEL BS	✓
EDEXCEL BC	✓
OCR BS	✓
OCR BCS	✓
WJEC BS	✓
CCEA BS	✗

The way that information is presented can be as important as the content it contains. Information that is presented effectively in a visual form will have an appropriate...

- **display**
- level of **detail**
- **method** of presentation (for the information and the users)
- set of **labels** to describe factors such as the information source, headings, and units used.

> 'NVC' (page 141) is the most common form of visual communication used in business.

Tables

Tables are widely used to summarise and display numerical information. The purpose of using a table is to group and organise the numerical information to make it more understandable. Tables often have the **source** and **date** of the information given.

Figure 8.5 Employees in jobs paid below the National Minimum Wage (NMW) 2008 (extract)
(Source: Labour Force Survey 2008)

	Jobs paid below NMW		Total jobs		Percentage of jobs paid below the NMW
	Thousands	Percentage	Thousands	Percentage	
Men	169	38	13 257	51	1.3
Women	275	62	12 857	49	2.1
Full-time	154	35	18 914	72	0.8
Part-time	291	65	7 200	28	4.0

Tables are effective at displaying **summarised numerical information** accurately and concisely although they lack the visual appeal of charts and graphs.

Graphs and charts

Graphs plot values at points that are joined together and can therefore be effective at showing **trends**. There are many types of **charts** – pie charts and bar charts are two common forms – that typically use the **size of shapes** to display similar information.

The graph on page 144 from the National Statistics website – www.statistics.gov.uk – illustrates how graphs can compare different items (in this example, two ways to measure inflation).

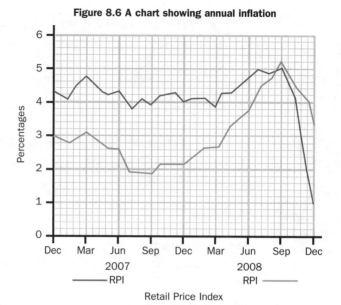

Figure 8.6 A chart showing annual inflation

The following bar chart summarises how things such as prices vary from region to region.

Figure 8.7 A chart showing how price levels vary regionally (Source: National Statistics 2008)

Here is a pie chart illustrating how dwellings vary in type.

Figure 8.8 A chart showing the type of dwellings in the UK. Source: National Census 2001

To communicate visually, businesses also use photographs, flowcharts and other diagrams, maps and plans

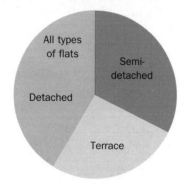

KEY POINT

Visual communication is often used where **impact** is required to 'get the message across'.

PROGRESS CHECK

1. What are the two main types of oral communication?
2. What is the difference between an agenda for, and minutes of, a meeting?

2. Agenda shows the business to be conducted; minutes summarise what was said.
1. Face-to-face; telephone.

8.3 Successful business communication

LEARNING SUMMARY

After studying this section you should be able to understand:

- the main barriers that stop communication being successful
- the impact that successful communication has on a business
- the impact of poor communication on stakeholders

Barriers to successful communication

AQA BS	✗
AQA BCS	✓
EDEXCEL BS	✓
EDEXCEL BC	✓
OCR BS	✓
OCR BCS	✓
WJEC BS	✓
CCEA BS	✓

The effectiveness of business communication is influenced by its main elements: the sender, the message, the medium and the recipient.

The **sender** could use...
- inaccurate technical terms or specialist vocabulary
- summaries that miss out important information
- an inappropriate level of language, e.g. jargon or over-complex terms
- over-long sentences or poor sentence structure.

Figure 8.9 An example of over-complicated language

"If there are any of these points about which you need explanation or further particulars we shall be pleased to furnish these additional details as may be requested by telephone."

(in other words: If you have any questions, please ring.)

The **message** could be sent...
- over a long chain of command (page 55), which leads to it being transmitted through too many people and levels
- containing far more information than is needed
- between a sender and a recipient who are quite different, e.g. in background or culture.

The **medium** could be...
- unsuitable for the information being sent
- too slow to get the message to the recipient in time for it to be acted upon.

The **recipient** could...
- have poor listening or reading skills
- interpret the message in a way that was not intended, e.g. due to personal bias or a wish to hear or read something else
- be in an unsuitable state (e.g. being upset or annoyed) to receive the message accurately.

There is the additional problem of '**noise**' – anything that stops the message being transmitted clearly. Examples of 'noise' include actual noise (e.g. in a factory), and faulty equipment so the message is not sent correctly.

Figure 8.10 External noise can distort the message being sent

The importance of successful communication

AQA BS	X
AQA BCS	✓
EDEXCEL BS	✓
EDEXCEL BC	✓
OCR BS	✓
OCR BCS	✓
WJEC BS	✓
CCEA BS	✓

Successful communication is necessary to a business because of the relationship it has with its various **stakeholders** (page 25). Good communication will help to...
- **explain its mission** – so all stakeholders can understand its purpose and goals
- build a **good reputation** for the business – so the local community will welcome its presence near them
- **increase sales** – customers will be dealt with efficiently and advertising and promotion will be effective, which helps create and maintain customer interest
- **motivate staff** – managers and other employees will benefit from efficient communication systems, and well-informed staff will work more efficiently
- improve the **quality of product information** – to support customers, who are more likely to make repeat orders.

Fig.8.11 Cats Protection, clear communication of its mission and objectives

Our vision is to ensure that every cat is given the chance of a life where it will be treated with kindness and an understanding of its needs.

Cats Protection has simple and clear objectives to help cats:
- **Homing** – finding good homes for cats in need
- **Neutering** – supporting and encouraging the neutering of cats
- **Information** – improving people's understanding of cats and their care

The effect of poor communication

Poor communication with stakeholders increases costs, damages the reputation of the business, and reduces its productivity and efficiency. Stakeholders are affected in a number of ways, for example:

● **Customers** lose interest and patience with the business, so sales fall because repeat orders are not made.

● **Suppliers** stop trading with the business, which then faces problems in continuing to produce its goods or services.

● The **local community** loses confidence and trust in the business, which then gains a bad reputation and faces difficulty in recruiting local people.

● **Employees** become unmotivated, which affects their work efficiency and the overall productivity for the business.

● **Lenders** such as banks become less willing to lend to the business, which can lead to problems with its **liquidity** (page 95).

Figure 8.12 Poor communication leads to business disputes

KEY POINT

Poor communication with stakeholders leads to loss of business

PROGRESS CHECK

1 State four influences on the effectiveness of business communication

2 Outline one way in which successful communication is important to an organisation

2. **Any suitable answer, e.g.** It will help to motivate the organisation's employees.

1. The sender, the message, the medium and the recipient.

8.4 Communicating with stakeholders

After studying this section you should be able to understand:

- examples of oral communication with stakeholders
- the nature of formal written communication with stakeholders
- how businesses communicate visually with stakeholders

Types of oral communication with stakeholders

AQA BS	✗
AQA BCS	✓
EDEXCEL BS	✓
EDEXCEL BC	✓
OCR BS	✓
OCR BCS	✓
WJEC BS	✓
CCEA BS	✓

Face-to-face meetings

Face-to-face meetings give businesses the opportunity to **achieve their mission and aims** and to **help and support stakeholders** who attend.

Meetings are important for communication. A well run and relevant meeting should help stakeholders by saving time, increasing motivation and productivity, providing information and solving problems. Meetings also encourage new ideas and initiatives.

> A face-to-face meeting overcomes problems and personal concerns in a way that written contact such as emails and memos cannot.

> 'Virtual meetings' (page 165) are a recent development that allow face-to-face contact.

Meetings are effective because of the **limitations of written communication**. Research suggests that communication by the written word carries less that 10 percent of the true meaning and feeling of the content. Face-to-face meetings are also more effective than other non-visual forms (such as a telephone conference) because only about 40 percent of the true meaning and feeling of the communication comes from what is said: the rest of the meaning and feeling – the majority – comes from **non-verbal communication** (page 141).

An **Annual General Meeting (AGM)** of an organisation – often a public company – may have to be held by law or because of the organisation's rules. An AGM is normally held each year. It allows the directors or managers to **inform the organisation's members of past activities and future activities**. The organisation's officers – for example, the directors of a public limited company (and its auditors) – are normally elected at the AGM.

Since 2007, private companies no longer have to hold an AGM

Notice of the AGM is sent out in advance. Figure 8.12 is a typical Notice of AGM with the meeting's contents listed.

Figure 8.12 Notice calling an AGM

Notice of Sanco plc

Annual General Meeting 2009
11.00 a.m. on 24 July 2009
Warwickshire Motor Museum,
Birmingham Road, Burnhill, Coventry

Contents

1. To receive the Directors' Report and Accounts
2. To approve the Directors' Remuneration Report
3. To declare a final dividend
4. To re-elect the following persons as directors:
   Mr D Hodson
   Ms A Sharma
   Mr P Singleton
   Ms M Toblinski
5. To re-appoint the auditors
6. To set the auditors' remuneration
7. To authorise political donations by the Company and its subsidiaries

Appraisals (page 110) are another important form of face-to-face meeting, with the employee being the stakeholder. The main objectives of holding appraisals are usually to **review employees' performance and potential**. Appraisals benefit both employer and employees by **improving job performance**, helping to **identify strengths and weaknesses**, and **assessing the employee's development needs**.

> **KEY POINT**
>
> The aim of an effective meeting is that whatever the subject, the attendees feel that it took care of their needs as well as the agenda items.

Telephone calls

In business, the telephone is used for many purposes. For example to...

- give information
- answer questions
- plan activities
- buy and sell
- make a complaint.

> Giving out information over the telephone involves different skills to a face-to-face meeting

The telephone is often the main communication source and contact for an external stakeholder. As a result, the business person using the telephone represents the business to the outside world, and creates an impression of the business. The following aspects are important when communicating by phone.

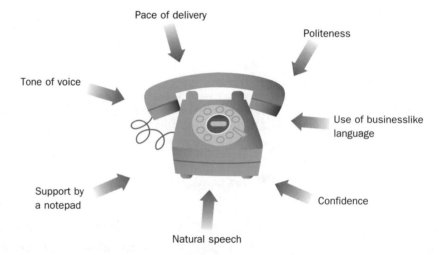

Specialist written communication

AQA BS	✗
AQA BCS	✓
EDEXCEL BS	✓
EDEXCEL BC	✓
OCR BS	✓
OCR BCS	✓
WJEC BS	✓
CCEA BS	✓

In addition to the normal written business communication such as letters and memos, there is sometimes the need to provide written communication in a special form. The most common example of this is a company's **annual report**. Figure 8.4 (page 141) shows the typical contents of an annual report. The Report contains key information for investors and other interested readers.

Figure 8.13 Extract from the Chief Executive's statement (Marks and Spencer's Annual Report 2008)

In 2004 we put in place a three-part plan for renewing and reinvigorating M&S in order to secure profitable growth and build the business for the long term. Our focus was on getting the basics right, by improving the products we offer, our customer service and shopping environments.

In 2007/08 we continued to make progress against the plan. We sold more goods to more people, reporting our biggest volume increase in sales in eight years, with volume market share in clothing and footwear at 11.2%. At the same time, we held our lead in the value market for clothing and footwear achieving 11.0% market share. Clothing and home sales were up 1.4% to almost £4.06bn. Per una also performed strongly under the leadership of George Davies, reporting sales of more than £428m.

In food, a good performance saw sales increase from £3.97bn to almost £4.25bn, and value market share remain steady at 4.3%.

Images used to communicate with stakeholders

AQA BS	✗
AQA BCS	✓
EDEXCEL BS	✓
EDEXCEL BC	✓
OCR BS	✓
OCR BCS	✓
WJEC BS	✓
CCEA BS	✓

Businesses use **visual communication methods** to communicate with their stakeholders. Much visual communication uses two-dimensional (2D) images. Logos, designs, adverts and the Internet are the most common forms of visual communication used in business.

A **logo** is an emblem or image that forms a business's trademark or brand. The use of **font**, **shape** and **colour** together help to create a logo that is immediately recognisable, and gives the organisation something to use in its advertising, promotion and as part of its image.

Figure 8.14 The Red Cross and Red Crescent logos are easily recognisable

> A registered design is a valuable asset for a business

A **design** (page 17) is about the way a product (or other object) looks. A business can **register** its product design, which protects it from unauthorised copying by a competitor. Once a design is registered, the business owning the design has a legal right that protects the visual appearance of its product in the area where it is registered.

Advertisements (page 71) help to create brand image and brand loyalty with the business's customers. **The Internet** allows businesses to create and use 2D visual adverts and other displays to inform and persuade both surfers and their stakeholders (such as customers).

Figure 8.15 The website of the publishers Letts Educational and Lonsdale

KEY POINT

Visual images help to communicate the image, aims and mission of a business.

PROGRESS CHECK

1. Give two ways in which a well run meeting helps stakeholders.
2. What is the purpose of an Annual General Meeting?

1. Increases their motivation; provides information for them.
2. An AGM is held to inform members of what has happened in the organisation and what is planned to happen in the future.

Sample GCSE questions

This question is about the value of efficient communication.

Asif Patel owns *FarmFresh Foods*, a small store in his local town centre that sells fruit and vegetables. Asif works in the business during the week and employs help on Saturdays, his busiest day. A large supermarket has just opened on a new 'out-of-town' retail park site, and Asif realises he will face increased competition. Asif also realises how important it is to have efficient communication with his employees, customers and the local community.

(a) Here are four examples of communication methods used by Asif.

'Post-it' notes   Talking during tea-breaks   Business letter   Meeting

Which two of these are examples of **(i) formal** communication; **(ii) informal** communication?

Business letters and meetings are formal methods; post-it notes and talking during tea-breaks are informal. **(2)**

(b) Explain the benefits to Asif that come from efficient communication with his customers and the local community.

By having efficient communication, customers and his local community will know what he sells in his shop and will be more likely to buy from there. Because Asif now has more competition, he needs to communicate what he sells and any offers on the products such as price bargains. They will also know when his shop is open, and where it is, if communication (e.g. advertising) is effective. **(4)**

(c) How might efficient internal and external communication help Asif's business to compete with the newly opened supermarket? Support your answer with relevant examples.

Internal communication such as using memos and a notice board mean that Asif's employees will understand what is going on. They will be able to deal with customers more efficiently. External methods such as business letters, phone calls and adverts will lead to efficient relationships with key stakeholders such as suppliers and customers. **(6)**

Good answer, all correct.

Good points made, but the answer could be improved by pointing out that Asif's customers are likely to live in the local community. Repeat purchases are an important feature of small-shop trade, so refer to this in the answer.

Good examples but 'what is going on' is vague: 'employees will understand and be up-to-date with issues such as the increased competition' is stronger.

A good point but develop by mentioning they will be more motivated so customer service will benefit.

Good examples and a good start with effective use of 'stakeholders'. Develop by exlaining how adverts or phone calls improve sales and inform customers, to counteract the supermarket.

Sample GCSE questions

This question is about internal and external communication and their methods.

Sandy Podgbury owns *Sandy's Sports Store*, a shop that sells sports equipment. Sandy employs two full-time and three-part-time members of staff to help.

(a) **(i)** Suggest an example of an internal communication method that Sandy is likely to use in *Sandy's Sports Store*.

An example of internal communication is meetings. **(1)**

(ii) Suggest an example of an external communication method that Sandy is likely to use in *Sandy's Sports Store*.

An example of external communication is business memos. **(1)**

(b) Sandy is a member of her local Chamber of Commerce. Before each meeting, Sandy is sent an agenda for the meeting together with minutes of the previous meeting.

(i) Why should an agenda always be sent to members of the meeting before it is due to take place?

An agenda should be sent so that members going to the meeting know what is going to be discussed at the meeting. **(2)**

(ii) List four items that Sandy would expect to see on the agenda.

Apologies for absence. When the meeting is to take place (the date). Minutes of the last meeting. Any other business. **(4)**

(iii) Why must the minutes of the previous meeting be correct and accurate?

Because if Sandy (or anyone else) couldn't go, they can find out exactly what was said and done at the meeting. **(2)**

(c) Sandy communicates regularly with her staff in *Sandy's Sports Store*. Outline two problems that could arise if Sandy's communication with these employees is of a poor standard.

Her employees will not know what to do when they are serving customers. They will be stressed and therefore not good in the shop. **(6)**

This is a suitable example.

No. Memos are classed as internal methods; a business letter is a better example.

Quite a good answer but it could be strengthened by mentioning that the members can organise themselves, e.g. by collecting together and bringing any relevant papers for the meeting.

All are correct though 'the date' could be expanded to mention the time as well.

A good answer, though 'done' could be improved by substituting 'agreed'.

The start of a good answer but expand both points. If employees do not know 'what to do' this will result in fewer sales and poor quality customer service. If 'stressed and not good in the shop' they will not be motivated (better than 'stressed') and will not know information about sports goods (a clearer phrase than 'not good in the shop'), and customers will go elsewhere.

Exam practice questions

This is a question on the use of business letters.

1 Carla Offe works in the HR Department of *Gosee plc*, a large company. Carla deals with application forms for posts at the company, and she sends letters to all short-listed applicants inviting them for interview.

Lou Beller works in the Public Relations Department of *Gosee plc*. It is Lou's responsibility to reply to people who write to *Gosee plc* with complaints or concerning other matters to do with the company. It is the policy of *Gosee plc* to reply by letter to every person who has written to the company.

(a) Why is a letter an appropriate form of communication in both situations above?

....

....

....

.... **(4)**

Carla is in charge of Blasko, a recent starter at *Gosee plc*. Carla has asked Blasko to write a memo to all departmental team leaders asking them to attend a training session on new equipment. Blasko has drafted the following text for the memo.

> This memo is to in form you that next month we will be holding a training sesion for you to know about some new equipment stuff we have bought.
>
> The training sesions will be held hear in the Training Office and we will be in touch again with a list of dates to sea witch suit you.
>
> Please contact my boss Carla Off if you have any queiries.

(b) **(i)** Correct any spelling errors in the above memo.

....

.... **(4)**

(ii) Suggest any improvements that could be made to the memo's content as it stands.

....

.... **(4)**

(iii) Identify two other items of information that will need to go in this memo.

....

.... **(2)**

9 ICT support for business

The following topics are covered in this chapter:

- **Administration**
- **The work environment**
- **Support for the work environment**
- **ICT knowledge and skills**

9.1 Administration

LEARNING SUMMARY

After studying this section you should be able to understand:

- the nature and role of administration
- how data needs to be secure
- the main points of data protection law

The nature of administration

AQA BS	✗
AQA BCS	✓
EDEXCEL BS	✗
EDEXCEL BC	✓
OCR BS	✓
OCR BCS	✓
WJEC BS	✗
CCEA BS	✗

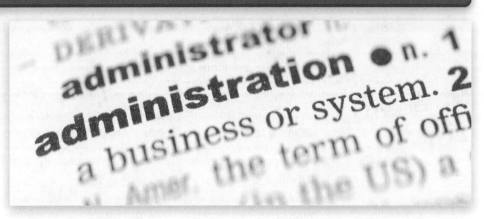

Records need to be kept and communicated in business, for example, information on employees, products, stocks, and contracts. There must be a system of record-keeping that allows the **information to be stored, processed, retrieved and transmitted**. The administration function is most closely associated with these tasks. Efficient administration helps the business run efficiently, making it more competitive.

An efficient storage and retrieval system used in administration needs these qualities:

- It must be capable of being **expanded** when necessary.
- It must be **easily understood** by its users.
- The information must be **easily accessible**.
- It must be **secure** from those who aren't entitled to use it.
- The information must be **safe from deterioration**.

Administrative tasks vary in their frequency and complexity. There is a difference for employees between **routine tasks** such as creating, sending and filing business documents, **and non-routine tasks**, – for example, being involved with product or market development. Employees must be able to deal with both types of tasks and will have to **prioritise** those tasks that are particularly important or urgent.

When preparing, storing and retrieving files – electronic and paper based – and other information, **accuracy** is important. Business documents need to be **checked for errors** in order to correct them. A lack of accuracy, and unprofessional presentation of business documents, will discourage external stakeholders such as customers and suppliers from continuing to trade with the business. The use of inaccurate information about internal stakeholders such as employees is likely to affect morale and motivation, which will lower employee productivity and output.

Security of data

Data exists in business in different forms, for example, text, numerical and graphical. It is also created by a variety of internal and external sources. Personal and financial information is most frequently created from the data collected.

Whatever the nature, type and source, it is important in the workplace to **keep data secure**. Commonly found hazards include destruction by physical means – for example, a fire at the premises – or by electronic means such as computer viruses.

Data must be protected physically, electronically, and from unauthorised access. **Physical protection** includes access rights – e.g. controlled access by locking doors, and alarm signals – and the use of fireproof storage units. There are many different methods used to protect **electronic** data from corruption or unauthorised access. These include the following:

- **Firewalls** – systems that can be set up in hardware, software, or both to prevent unauthorised users accessing a private network. Firewalls are best known for stopping Internet users from gaining access to private networks, particularly intranets.
- **Anti-virus software** – this identifies and removes computer viruses and **malware** (harmful computer software that includes Trojans, worms and phishing attacks).
- **Anti-spam** techniques – software and other techniques that reject spam emails whilst allowing legitimate emails to be accessed.
- **Anti-spyware** software – these programs, often linked to anti-virus software, are designed to remove or block spyware software that seeks to collect information on Internet users and can change computer settings.

- **Encryption** – information format is changed using an algorithm to make it unreadable to anyone except those who have the 'key' that makes the information readable again.
- **Usernames** and **passwords** – user accounts are set up requiring computer users to identify themselves by name: a password, a secret word or series of letters and numbers known only to the user, also normally needs entering before computer access is allowed.

Figure 9.1 Password protection

The Data Protection Act 1998

'Data subjects' – people about whom the data is kept – have the right of access to their personal data.

The Data Protection Act covers how information about living people is used by protecting personal data held on computers or in an organised paper filing system. **Personal data** includes name, address and banking details. **Sensitive personal data** includes subjects such as a person's religion, health and political opinions. More safeguards are provided for sensitive data. The **Principles** of the Act include...

- data must be held and used for a registered purpose
- the amount of information must be adequate but not too much for the purpose for which it is being held
- information must be accurate and kept up to date
- information must also be held securely (e.g. by backing up and kept from unauthorised access)
- information must not be kept for longer than is necessary.

KEY POINT

Administration supports the other main functions of a business

PROGRESS CHECK

1. State two qualities that an efficient storage and retrieval system needs.
2. Give two examples of how data held electronically can be protected.

1. **Any two from:** Capable of expansion; easily accessible; easily understood; secure; safe from deterioration.
2. **Any two from:** Passwords; anti-virus software; firewalls; anti-spam; anti-spyware; encryption.

9.2 The work environment

LEARNING SUMMARY

After studying this section you should be able to understand:

- the main types of work environment
- ergonomics and other developments in the work environment
- the legal framework that affects work in its environment

Types of work environment

AQA BS	X
AQA BCS	✓
EDEXCEL BS	X
EDEXCEL BC	X
OCR BS	✓
OCR BCS	✓
WJEC BS	X
CCEA BS	X

Work is carried out in different kinds of working environments. Popular examples include:

- **Open plan** offices – employee desks are located in a large building. This gives limited privacy (e.g. by the use of standing screens) but treats all employees equally and encourages teamwork.
- **Cellular** offices – having individual 'closed office' space. This gives employees confidential and private working space but promotes individualism rather than teamwork and co-operation.

> It is important to position desks and organise working space to maximise work quality and efficiency.

An open plan office

Developments in workplace organisation

> 'Home working' is a type of teleworking. It cuts travel time and costs and so reduces the environmental impact of work.

Flexible working refers to work arranged to suit the individual employee, for example, part-time working, 'flexi-time' working and job sharing. **Teleworking** – when ICT enables work to be done away from the place where the work results are used – gives employees the freedom to organise their own work environment and reduces the business's need for traditional office space.

The growth in part-time work has encouraged the use of **hot-desking** – each desk is used by different employees at different times. This reduces the space the business pays for (and therefore its costs). However, some employees value their own space and do not like sharing it with colleagues.

Ergonomics

The science of ergonomics uses information about human movement when objects and systems (such as workplace systems) are being designed. **Ergonomic design** is used at work to examine different design options, choosing the ones that best support the employees. This helps to ensure that workplace environment systems and equipment are efficient and fit for use by the employees.

The importance of ergonomic design

KEY POINT

The type of workplace organisation is influenced by the type and requirements of the business and the tasks carried out

The legal framework

AQA BS	✗
AQA BCS	✓
EDEXCEL BS	✗
EDEXCEL BC	✗
OCR BS	✓
OCR BCS	✓
WJEC BS	✗
CCEA BS	✗

There are many different laws that influence how work is carried out in its environment. These laws include...

- data protection (page 157)
- health and safety at work (page 121)
- consumer protection (pages 37–38)
- copyright (page 17)
- employment law (pages 119–121).

There are other laws and regulations that influence the work environment:

- The **Freedom of Information Act** gives people the right to request **access to information** held by public authorities (the Environmental Information Regulations give people similar rights to access environmental information). Not all information will be released, for example, information will be withheld if its release would affect national security or damage commercial interests.
- **Electronic communication** is controlled by the **Privacy and Electronic Communications Regulations** which controls organisations that send electronic direct marketing, e.g. by email. Any direct marketing by phone, email, text or other electronic means that is unsolicited (not requested by the recipient) is strictly regulated. Recipients can object to electronic marketing and can register with a preference service to stop their names and addresses being accessed by senders.

- The **Computer Misuse Act** makes unauthorised access to computer systems a criminal offence. The offences are accessing computer material without permission and with intent to commit further offences (hacking), and changing computer data without permission, e.g. introducing a virus to destroy data.
- **Environmental protection.** The **Waste, Electrical and Electronic Equipment (WEEE) Directive** seeks to reduce the amount of electrical and electronic equipment being produced and to encourage everyone to reuse, recycle and recover it. The WEEE Directive also seeks to improve the environmental performance of businesses that make, supply, use and recycle this equipment.

Figure 9.3 The WEEE Directive

KEY POINT

The choice of work environment is influenced by factors such as the amount of noise being created, or the sensitivity of the information being handled.

PROGRESS CHECK

1. What is 'flexible working'?
2. State the purpose of the Computer Misuse Act.

2. The Act makes unauthorised access to computer systems a criminal offence.
1. Work that is arranged to suit the individual employee.

9.3 Support for the work environment

LEARNING SUMMARY

After studying this section you should be able to understand:

- the variety of computers in work
- how electronic communications support work
- the effects of changing systems in work

Computers in work

AQA BS	✓
AQA BCS	✓
EDEXCEL BS	✗
EDEXCEL BC	✓
OCR BS	✓
OCR BCS	✓
WJEC BS	✓
CCEA BS	✓

ICT (Information and Communications Technology) allows businesses to store, protect, retrieve, process and transmit information. **Computers** – hardware, data input, storage and output – and **electronic communications** are key elements of ICT used in work.

Computer hardware

The most popular types of computer hardware includes desktop computers and networks, portable computers such as laptops and Personal Digital Assistants (PDAs), and electronic point of sale (EPOS) equipment.

EPOS 'electronic point of sale' equipment is widely used in any retailing location where a transaction occurs. For example, when buying meals in a restaurant or 'fast food' outlet, an EPOS system speeds up operations. It can connect to a 'store controller' server and printer, and monitor sales and other business data.

The main features of **desktop** and **laptop** computers include a monitor or screen, keyboard, a central processing unit (CPU) on a motherboard. The main difference is in use, with laptop computers having a rechargeable battery and designed for mobile use, giving the laptop a significant advantage over desktop computers. Other advantages of laptops over desktops include connectivity (e.g. the use of wireless networks and **dongles**), size, immediacy, i.e. instant access to information, and lower power consumption.

The **PDA** handheld computer – sometimes called a Palmtop computer – can often be used for a variety of purposes, such as a mobile phone, web browser and media player. Uses include vehicle navigation (e.g. global positioning systems) and record keeping such as electric and gas meter reading.

A Point of Sale transaction   The convenience of a laptop   The PDA

Data input devices

Keyboards, pointing devices, imaging and video devices, optical mark recognition (OMR) and optical character recognition (OCR) systems, voice recognition software and digital cameras are commonly used input devices.

- **Keyboards** have a layout based on keys being pressed either to input data or to access a computer function.
- **Pointing devices** allow users to input data usually by detecting movement (e.g. touch screens and mice). Other pointing devices such as touch screens and light pens allow data to be input directly.

Keyboards   Input by touch screen

The use of EPOS has increased efficiency of ordering, and lowered service times.

More laptops are now sold than desktops.

Input devices provide data and control signals to a computer

Reading the barcode

- **Imaging** and **video** devices such as image scanners and barcode readers digitise information to input into the computer. **Optical mark recognition** (OMR) captures data by shining beams of light on paper to scan and detect marked areas – less bright than the unmarked areas – that provide the data required. **Optical character recognition** (OCR) translates written or printed text – usually captured by a scanner – into text readable by a computer: a popular variation is magnetic ink character recognition, typically used on bank cheques.
- **Voice recognition software** programs work by analysing sounds and converting them to text. Noise levels and other factors will influence the quality and efficiency of any voice recognition system.
- **Digital cameras** capture photographs and video, which can then be imported into computers.

> Voice recognition software is are often used to control access to secure systems.

Data storage devices

Hard disk drives, CD / DVD drives, and high capacity storage devices such as memory sticks are mass and off-line storage devices that are widely used in business.

- **Hard disk** drives provide mass storage of data.
- **Flash memory** a non-volatile (power is not needed to keep the information stored) **USB memory stick** is now commonly being used. These storage devices have largely replaced **floppy disk** drives due to their advantages of being smaller, faster and capable of storing more information.
- **CD / DVD drives** are popular storage devices because CDs are portable, have a reasonably large storage capacity, are flexible (capable of storing video and audio) and can be created as read-only.

> Portable hard disk drives are commonly used to back up important files.

Data output devices

Monitors, projectors and printers are popular forms of output device.

- **Monitors** display computer output, having the advantage of being able to display movement (video) supported by sound, as well as text, but with the disadvantage that there is no permanent record of this output. Most monitors have a power-saving mode if no input is being received.

> Some printers can also scan and photocopy documents.

- **Printers** produce a **hard copy**, usually as a document from a computer as the source, though many printers now read data from other sources such as memory sticks. **Network printers** support all users on the network. Printers are most efficient when used for low-volume work with a short turnaround time. However, they are slow output devices, have a high cost per page printed, and have a high environmental cost (e.g. the use of paper and ink).
  - Laser printers can print rapidly high quality text and graphics, producing the image by scanning a laser beam.
  - Thermal printers are fed with heat-sensitive paper, heating parts of the paper to produce the image.
  - Inkjet printers use ink fed from cartridges to produce the image.
  - Toner-based printers add toner to a light-sensitive part such as a drum, use static electricity to transfer the toner to the paper, and seal it through heat.
- **Video projectors** receive video signals from a computer and project images on a screen. They are often used for demonstrations and training presentations.

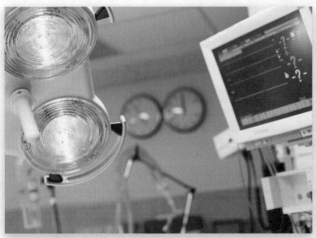

Using a monitor to display a patient's progress

Computer hardware, input, storage and output

Electronic communications in work

AQA BS	✓
AQA BCS	✓
EDEXCEL BS	✗
EDEXCEL BC	✓
OCR BS	✓
OCR BCS	✓
WJEC BS	✓
CCEA BS	✓

An online presence

The Internet has created many business opportunities. Having an online presence through a website allows a business to...

- inform customers about the business, its goods and services
- enable customers to place orders and pay for purchases
- offer their goods and services to a wider market
- communicate with, and send information to, its other stakeholders
- increase the amount and variety of advertising and promotion.

The business website will have a **domain name** – the unique name that identifies an Internet site – and use a **web hosting service**, which ensures its website can be accessed on the Internet.

When creating the business website authors must take into account factors such as...

- the amount of finance budgeted for the website
- the type and volume of information to be displayed
- the likely users of the website.

The business's website will be subject to a number of laws. These include **sale and supply of goods** (page 37), **data protection** (page 157) and **copyright** (page 17).

Figure 9.4 Information for students on the Letts Educational Ltd website

The success of a business website can be measured in various ways, including...

- sales from its e-commerce operation
- increased market share
- improved brand awareness
- a fall in the number of calls requesting help or support.

However, the Internet brings increased risks to a business as a result of the threat of **increased competition**. Websites also bring **additional costs** such as maintaining and updating the web pages, obtaining security systems and software to prevent unauthorised access and theft of customer information, and providing customer support outside the traditional working hours.

Email

Email involves creating, sending and storing information electronically. The computer server accepts, stores and forwards messages in text format, sometimes supported by attachments containing information in a variety of formats such as video and audio.

In business, email was the first 'e-revolution' in communication:

- Business users find email **easy to use**.
- Business users can **receive and download mail when offline**.
- Email is **inexpensive** – business users can contact multiple users using a single email and with a single connection.
- It is a **quick** communication method – there is almost instantaneous transmission of information.

However, there are drawbacks of using email in business:

- **Inappropriate** use of resources (some employees might misuse the business email facility, using it for personal rather than business purposes) and of language (when the writer fails to appreciate that emails in a business context are different from emails sent in a personal context).
- **Increasing** use – due to its ease of use, email correspondence sometimes dominates the work of an employee to the detriment of other work.
- Information **overload** – staff cannot cope with the volume of email information.

Other forms

Other forms of electronic communication include:

- **Video conferencing**, which uses a camera and microphone to send images and sound across a computer network, allowing communication nationally or internationally.
- **Teleconferencing**, which normally uses telephone lines to hold national or international discussions. In both cases, staff travel and time is saved and costs reduced.
- Although they have been largely replaced by mobile phones, **pagers** still offer a quick and reliable form of messaging, and will work in times of emergency.
- **Fax** machines, which are still used to transmit copies of business documents electronically, often using the telephone network. It has the advantage of immediate transmission, and fax machines can be left on '24/7' to receive documents outside normal work hours.
- **Podcast** audio and video information, distributed over the Internet, which allows broadcasters and other businesses to communicate with their clients.
- **Mobile phones** – people used to telephone a location but now, thanks to mobile phones, they can telephone a person. This allows employees to stay in touch more easily, for example when travelling. The **Short Message Service** (SMS) form of text messaging on mobile phones is an inexpensive way of contacting employees and other stakeholders.

Video conferencing

Mobile phones

Assessing ICT systems

AQA BS	✓
AQA BCS	✓
EDEXCEL BS	✗
EDEXCEL BC	✓
OCR BS	✓
OCR BCS	✓
WJEC BS	✓
CCEA BS	✓

Many factors influence the effectiveness of a business ICT-based system:

- **Ease of use** – the system should be capable of being understood by the users, with little or no training.
- **Fitness for purpose** – the system should serve the purpose for which it is intended, and should contribute towards the organisation meeting its objectives.
- **Cost** – start-up and running costs should not be excessive, and the benefits from using the system should outweigh its costs.
- **Security** – there should be no unauthorised access to the system and its contents.
- **Health and safety** – the use of the equipment should not cause injury to employees, and should not cause sickness problems in the long term.
- Effect on the **environment** – it should not use more resources than necessary and it should have environmentally-friendly facilities such as an 'energy saving mode' built in.

Changing the system

Figure 9.5 Technology influences work and leads to change

ICT-based and other types of business communication systems need reviewing regularly by managers to see whether they can be developed or improved. Actions that managers must take include **reviewing** the existing system to identify areas that can be improved, **planning** the changes to the existing system, **implementing** the changes needed to bring about improvement, and **judging** the effectiveness of the new system.

Employees will be affected by the changes made because there will be changes in...

- **roles and skills** – such as an increase in multi-tasking or a new responsibility for creating own documents
- **work practices** – e.g. home working, working whilst travelling
- **status** – e.g. new jobs, the offer of redundancy.

Employees may **resist change** for these reasons:

- **Job status** – if the change will lead to an employee losing power or responsibility.
- **Fear and insecurity** – many employees believe they will not be able to cope with the new systems.
- **Personal reasons** – employees resist changes that put them under pressure, for example by being asked to move job and / or area.

> There is greater job mobility because the pace of technological change leads to old jobs dying and new ones replacing them.

Figure 9.6 Resisting change

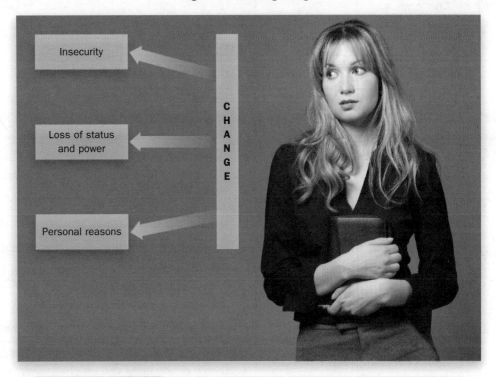

PROGRESS CHECK

1. Name three factors that help determine the efficiency of an ICT-based system.
2. State three reasons why an employee might resist change in the organisation.

1. How easy it is to use; its start-up and running costs; the quality of its security.
2. Reduced job status; fear of how the change will affect work role; personal reasons.

9.4 ICT knowledge and skills

LEARNING SUMMARY

After studying this section you should be able to understand:
● the range of knowledge and skills needed to use business software.

Applications software

AQA BS	✗
AQA BCS	✓
EDEXCEL BS	✗
EDEXCEL BC	✓
OCR BS	✓
OCR BCS	✓
WJEC BS	✗
CCEA BS	✗

The benefits of using word processing in business includes increased productivity, for example, through the use of standard letters - and improved presentation (more 'professional' communication with stakeholders). DTP packages cut business costs by creating documents such as advertising leaflets, price lists, menus and catalogues 'in-house'.

Application	Task	Skill
Word processing and Desk Top Publishing (DTP)	Business documents	• Create and input information with correct spelling, punctuation and grammar into documents such as letters, agendas, minutes, leaflets, using a suitable business layout
	Fonts, page layouts and graphics	• Use different font formats – e.g. by size, colour and type – and paragraph formats – e.g. indentation, alignment, spacing, numbering and bullet points • Use different page layouts – e.g. use of header and footer, tables, columns • Use suitable graphics – e.g. word art, pictures, drawings and diagrams • Combine text and graphics • Use suitable facilities – e.g. search and replace, thesaurus, moving text
Spreadsheet	Construction	• Format rows and columns • Input data accurately with descriptions such as headings • Input accurate and appropriate formulae and functions
	Use	• Carry out calculations – e.g. sum, average • Create charts using various chart formats with suitable labelling
Database	Construction	• Design suitable data capture documentation • Insert, delete and edit data fields
	Use	• Search and sort records using given criteria • Filter records and create reports
Graphics software	Use	• Create various shapes, supported by shading and patterns • Re-size graphics • Move graphics
Presentation software	Construction	• Create new slides using templates or blank slides • Format slide layout involving text and graphics • Insert and format or re-size text, numbers, graphics and animation • Print information
Web authoring	Construction	• Create web pages inputting information accurately • Use suitable font, colour and paragraph formats • Insert images and use animation • Create hyperlinks

KEY POINT

We hear a lot about the 'paperless office' but in reality paper is still an important medium of communication in business.

PROGRESS CHECK

1 Give two benefits associated with using word processing.
2 State two tasks required to construct a spreadsheet.

1. Increased productivity; improved presentation, or any other sensible answer.
2. Format rows and columns; enter formulae.

Sample GCSE questions

This is a question on storing and accessing data.

NKG Ltd employees use ICT for business. Each employee has a username and password.

(a) What is one advantage to *NKG Ltd* of giving each employee a username and password?

> It means not anyone can get on the computer. **(2)**

The computers at *NKG Ltd* store confidential and sensitive information about employees. It is only recently that *NKG Ltd* has installed a firewall and anti-virus software on its computer network.

(b) **(i)** Other than usernames and passwords, state one method that *NKG Ltd* might use to stop unauthorised access to this information.

> The computers containing this information could be kept in a separate locked room. **(1)**

(ii) Outline two risks that *NKG Ltd* no longer faces because of installing these items on the computers.

> It stops viruses being downloaded without anyone knowing. Also, it stops hackers (these are people who are not authorised to view what is on the computer) getting access to NKG Ltd's computer system. **(4)**

NKG Ltd used to transact business using paper-based systems. All correspondence used to be kept on paper and filed in filing cabinets. The company now keeps electronic copies only of all correspondence.

(c) **(i)** Explain the drawbacks to *NKG Ltd* of its old method of keeping records.

> This would have needed a lot of space, and more and more space would be needed as time went on because of the build-up of correspondence. Space means money, and of course the filing cabinets also cost a lot of money. There is also a greater fire risk because paper can be set alight very easily. Also, if paper files are kept, some items can be put in the wrong file and it would be very difficult and time consuming to find it. Files can also get lost easily. **(4)**

(ii) Give two benefits to *NKG Ltd* of keeping electronic copies only.

> Less space is needed, and the files can be easily accessed by many users. **(4)**

Exam practice questions

This question is based on administration and ICT in a business.

1 You work in the Administrative Department of *Sankea Ltd*, a company making and selling jewellery. *Sankea Ltd* sells jewellery in a chain of shops that it owns, and on its website. Your Manager is Lloyd Davies.

Lloyd has asked you to prepare a written report for the Sales Manager on jewellery sales made by each shop and over the Internet last year, month by month. Lloyd wants you to include charts and graphs in the report.

(a) Identify two types of computer software that will allow you to write the report and to include charts and graphs.

.... **(2)**

(b) The Sales Manager wants you to send copies of the completed report to each shop manager, by email attachment.

(i) Describe two advantages of using email, rather than the post, for this purpose.

....

.... **(4)**

(ii) List four steps you will need to follow to send the report by email after you have connected to the Internet and opened the email software.

....

.... **(4)**

(c) **(i)** State two benefits to *Sankea Ltd*, and two benefits to its customers, of using the website to sell the jewellery.

....

.... **(4)**

(ii) State one thing that a customer should check on this website to ensure it is a secure site.

.... **(1)**

Because it records details of customers who buy using its website, *Sankea Ltd* must obey the Principles of the Data Protection Act.

(d) Identify two Principles of this Act that *Sankea Ltd* must obey.

....

.... **(2)**

Exam practice answers

Chapter 1

1. **(a) (i)** To check that his business is viable and to help obtain finance and investment.
   (ii) Executive summary; Description of the business; Marketing strategy; Financial plan.
   (b) Choose his location, e.g. will he work at home or rent premises? Arrange finance – does he have the capital to start the business?
   (c) Two risks Ashok faces are: that the business will fail (financial risk of losing his investment); that he will not protect his invention (a competitor might copy and produce it at a lower price).
   (d) Initiative; Determination; Honesty; Creative thinking.
   (e) Patent the invention: Ashok's collar invention is a type of intellectual property and a patent will protect the collar from being copied by someone else who then produces it to compete with Ashok. As a result he can profit from his invention.

Chapter 2

1. **(a)** An ageing population: increase in the 46–64 and 65 and over age groups from 40% to 54%, and fall in the 45 and under segment from 60% to 46%. Since the younger age groups will soon comprise less than half the local population, compared with 3 in 5 at present, this will affect demand for the Centre's services (likely to be higher in the younger age range). There will also be a switch from sporting activities demanded by younger people (e.g. gymnasia) to the more leisure-based ones demanded by older people, or to sports they can undertake more gently (e.g. swimming). There may also be a change in demand for, and income from, membership.
   (b) The Centre should review its facilities to ensure it can adapt to these changing demands. It should also review how and where it advertises its services, and the type of membership it offers, to encourage a greater number of older people to join and attend.

Chapter 3

1.

A The company can have no more than 20 shareholders		**B** The company cannot sell shares to the general public		
C The company's shares are sold on the Stock Exchange	✓	**D** The company's name is followed by 'ltd'		
E The company is owned by the government		**F** The company has unlimited liability		
G The company must have at least £50 000 share capital	✓	**H** The company's name is followed by 'plc'	✓

2. **B** has unlimited liability and **F** shares the work and profits between the owners.

Chapter 4

1.

A Carrying out market research	✓	**B** Production planning	
C Paying suppliers		**D** Constructing accounts	
E Quality assurance		**F** Using advertising agencies	✓
G Selecting new staff		**H** Storing raw materials	
I Promoting sales	✓	**J** Ordering new machinery	

2. **A** Reading trade magazines and **C** Studying Government statistics

3. **(a)** 'Marketing mix' refers to product, price, place and promotion. In this example, the products are the food items made: perishable, either high-turnover (bread) or one-off/batch (cakes), items marketed to the public. Prices are based on cost-plus (bread) and skimming (cakes), and it uses loss leaders as part of its pricing policy to attract sales. 'Place' refers to the outlets, its own shops and catering establishments in the Midlands. Promotion is by loss leaders and advertising in local newspapers and at the point of sale.
   (b) 'Mass market' refers to a highly populated general market, such as the one for food products, e.g. bread. 'Loss leaders' occur where product lines are sold below cost to attract custom in the hope that consumers will also buy other items. 'Point-of-sale advertising' occurs at the point of sale (e.g. at a shop counter).
   (c) Bread is sold at 'cost-plus', when a percentage is added to the product's cost to get the selling price. Although this ensures production costs are met and there is a contribution towards overheads, competitors' prices are ignored, resulting in an uncompetitive price. Cakes are sold at a 'skimming' price, a high price that recognises the uniqueness of the product (or in this case there may be a local monopoly). This may encourage competitors to enter the local market, forcing the business to lower its prices to compete.
   (d) The company could use street surveys or in-store test marketing. Street surveys could be conducted close to local *SupaSlice* shops, thus surveying actual and potential consumers. Test marketing allows staff to talk to those already committed to buying its products: this gives direct feedback and is not expensive.

Chapter 5

1. **(a)** The output at which total costs and total revenue are the same.
   (b)

   Fixed costs per fair £300 (salary, rent, travel); selling price £30 so total revenue £900 at 30 paintings; variable costs £10 x 30 = £300 at 30 paintings so £600 total costs (300 + 300).
   (c) Break-even point shown on the graph is 15 paintings: £300 divided by (£30 – £10).
   (d) The graph shows £100 profit, difference between total revenue £600 and total costs £500.
   (e) (i) The main problems are likely to include: At present, insufficient equipment to make the numbers required for the new order; A limited amount of capital to invest in new equipment; A lack of storage and other space; A lack of time and staff to make the paintings.

Exam practice answers

(ii) Bill could consider obtaining larger premises (but there is the cost of buying / renting); Obtain additional equipment (but there is cost of buying / renting again); Arranging loans (but lender may want detailed financial statements; may not give loan); Take on a partner (need to find one; may not work well together; still have unlimited liability); Employ staff (may need training); Look to family / friends for capital (but may lead to domestic and friendship problems).

Chapter 6

1. **(a) (i)** A record of an individual's education, employment experience and other interests.
   (ii) Because the job requires up-to-date computer skills, so the company wants evidence of an applicant's ability to work with computers.
   (b) (i) Aptitude test: to check a candidate's suitability for the work, e.g. by providing a series of computer-based tests. Intelligence tests: to see if the candidate's intelligence is at the level expected for this position.
   (ii) The aptitude test will allow *Garfield Print* to compare the results of the candidates' work on computers, giving them valuable evidence, which they can use.
   (c) It allows candidates to explain any points the interviewers wish to ask. It allows both parties to make sure that the job is suitable for the candidate and that the candidate is suitable for the job.
   (d) (i) A contract of employment states the conditions under which the person is employed.
   (ii) Job title; names of both parties; rate of pay; holidays.

Chapter 7

1. **(a) (i)** An employee working in furniture production completes the whole item of furniture, i.e. works from start to finish on it.
   (ii) Advantage: Employees tend to be more interested in the work; Disadvantage: Slow method of production.
   (b) A larger output is made, allowing, for example, bulk buying of materials and efficient specialist equipment to be used. This means that the fixed costs for *Getbilt* are spread over a larger output, which reduces the average cost of production.
   (c) Flow production, assuming there is a sufficient market for the products. Job production if *Getbilt* is selling on the basis of 'quality', though this may be unlikely (because 'modern household furniture' suggests a mass market).

Chapter 8

1. **(a)** Carla: company has a permanent record; copying information to all applicants means all receive identical information; applicants have the letter for record / reference.
   Lou: company has a permanent record; could use standard letter to save time / resources; evidence of being sent; 'personal' reply to customers gives the company a good image.
   (b) (i) 'inform' not 'in form'; 'session' and 'sessions'; 'here'; 'see which'; 'Offe' not 'Off'; 'queries'.

(b) (ii) improve the phrase on line 2 e.g. 'for you to study some new equipment we...'; the words 'my boss' are not needed.
(b) (iii) the date of sending; contact details for Carla.

Chapter 9

1. **(a)** Word processor; spreadsheet.
   (b) (i) Low cost – less expensive than posting individual copies of the report, and saves printing cost. Immediate – quicker than by post.
   (b) (ii) Enter email address for each shop manager; select 'Add attachment'; search for and attach the report; press 'send'.
   (c) (i) *Sankea Ltd*: website is available '24/7'; gives the company a larger potential market. Customers: can buy without having to leave their house (convenience); can buy even if there is no local shop.
   (c) (ii) The 'padlock' icon is showing on the status bar.
   (d) Any two from: Personal data is to be obtained for specified lawful purposes; personal data must be accurate and (if necessary) kept up to date; the amount of information must be adequate; the information must be held securely.

Notes

173

Index

Index

Index

Acknowledgements

p10   ©Newcast: Virgin. www.newscast.com
p14   ©McDonalds: Used with the permission of McDonald's Restaurants Ltd
p15   ©BFA Logo: Used with the permission of the BFA: www.thebfa.org
p16   ©Amazon: Image Courtesy of Amazon.com, All Rights Reserved
p17   ©Newcast: Coca-Cola Company
       ©Cadbury: www.cadbury.co.uk
       ©Royal Mail: www.royalmail.com/ip
p 20   ©John Lewis: www.johnlewispartnership.co.uk
p26   ©Tesco: www.tescoplc.com
p29   ©iStockphoto.com / Joshua Blake
       ©iStockphoto.com
p31   ©Toyota: www.toyota.co.uk
       ©BMW: www.bmw.com
       ©Vauxhall: www.vauxhall.co.uk
p32   ©iStockphoto.com / Jonathan Scheele
       ©iStockphoto.com / JRussell Tate
       ©iStockphoto.com
p41   ©ABTA: www.abta.com
       ©RAC: www.racnews.co.uk
p42   ©Morrisons: www.morrisons.co.uk/corporate
p49   ©Marks and Spencer: www.marksandspencer.com
p50   ©Co-operative: www.co-operative.coop
p51   ©Tesco: www.tescoplc.com
p56   ©Tesco: www.tescoplc.com
p72   ©iStockphoto.com / JEdward Murphy;
       ©iStockphoto.com / JNicholas Monu
       ©iStockphoto.com / JJoshua Blake
p73   www.morrisons.co.uk
p77   www.jsainsburys.co.uk
p116   ©iStockphoto.com / Russell Tate
p142   ©iStockphoto.com / Julien Grondin
p146   ©www.cats.org.uk

p150   ©iStockphoto.com / Russell Tate
p151   ©International Federation of Red Cross and Red Crescent Societies, www.ifrc.or

All other images ©2009 Jupiterimages Corporation and Letts Educational Ltd.